AF242391

invite
PRESS

The Christian's Pattern

J. David Juliano

The Christian's Pattern

A Simple Guide to Follow Jesus Everyday

A modern daily devotional based on
John Wesley's adaptation
of the classic disciple guide
The Imitation of Christ
by Thomas á Kempis

invite PRESS
Plano, Texas

The Christian's Pattern:
A Simple Guide to Follow Jesus Everyday

Copyright © 2026 by J. David Juliano
All rights reserved.

No part of this work may be reproduced or transmitted in any form or by any means, electronic or mechanical, including photocopying and recording, or by any information storage or retrieval system, except as may be expressly permitted by the 1976 Copyright Act or in writing from the publisher. Requests for permission can be addressed to Permissions, Invite Press, P.O. Box 260917, Plano, TX 75026.

This book is printed on acid-free, elemental chlorine-free paper.

ISBN Paperback 9781971591001, eBook 9781963265934

Unless otherwise noted, all Scripture quotations are the author's own paraphrase, primarily sourced from the King James Version of the Bible and The Holy Bible, New International Version.

Scripture quotations marked NIV are taken from THE HOLY BIBLE, NEW INTERNATIONAL VERSION®, NIV® Copyright © 1973, 1978, 1984, 2011 by Biblica, Inc.™ Used by permission of Zondervan. All rights reserved worldwide.

26 27 28 29 30 31 32 33 34 35—10 9 8 7 6 5 4 3 2 1

MANUFACTURED IN THE UNITED STATES OF AMERICA

Table of Contents

THE CHRISTIAN'S PATTERN – BOOK THREE

THE CHRISTIAN'S PATTERN — BOOK FOUR

Introduction

I grew up with godly grandparents and great-grandparents, all steeped in generations of Methodist heritage. But I can't say I was especially aware of this as a child. I wouldn't have even recognized the name John Wesley. It wasn't until I was eighteen, having never been a regular churchgoer, that I realized something was missing in my life and began looking for a church home.

An anglophile since I was young enough to read *The Tales of King Arthur*, I thought I wanted to be an Episcopalian. Actually, to be precise, I was desperate to be an Episcopalian. But after three Sundays in a row of worshiping at the small Episcopal church in my hometown and not being spoken to or acknowledged, I reluctantly had to admit that maybe God didn't want me to be an Episcopalian.

It was then that I wandered into the First Methodist Church of Murfreesboro, Tennessee. I was met at the door by a giant of a man named Mr. Eugene Hoover with a broad smile, hands like catcher's mitts, and a welcoming demeanor. He wore the most amazing collection of diamond-studded Coke bottle lapel pins, having retired from our local Coca-Cola bottling plant. Mr. Hoover had me handing out bulletins and ringing the bell before I even joined the church. It was there at the First Methodist Church of Murfreesboro that I was introduced to and fell in love with the diminutive English cleric named John Wesley. I was captivated by the way God had raised him up and used him and his brother, Charles, to fuel the greatest revival the world had seen since the Book of Acts. I immersed myself in every biography I could find. It didn't take me long to relate to Wesley's faltering journey to faith, his struggles with works-righteousness, and his feeling that he never quite measured up.

I was struck by the books Wesley read during his early days, signposts that eventually led him to that prayer meeting on Aldersgate Street. Books like William Law's *A Serious Call to a Devout and Holy Life*, Jeremy Taylor's *Rules for Holy Living and Dying*, and, of course, *The Imitation of Christ* by Thomas à Kempis.

When God eventually called me to pastoral ministry, I read all of these books. Each of these authors painted a thrilling vision of a life fully devoted to God. But the book that stayed with me was à Kempis' *Imitation*. I knew that Wesley had edited and published a version for his own "Christian Library," but I had never read that specific edition. Still, the version I read during my college days remained on my study shelf for over thirty-five years.

My church recently gifted me with a sabbatical. Coming out of that sabbatical, I resolved to be more intentional about my daily devotional life. "Where do I start after years of fits and bursts?" My eye was immediately drawn to à Kempis' classic. I took it down and started reading a chapter a day.

The first thing that struck me was, "Wow, this is hard! How did I ever get through this, let alone derive any benefit from it as a young twenty-something?"

And then the idea hit me: Why not introduce modern-day Christians in the Wesleyan stream to John Wesley's translation of *The Imitation of Christ* in a way that is easy to read, accessible, and relevant to Christians living in a noisy, frenetic, post-modern world characterized by doomscrolling and sound bites?

That's what you're holding in your hands.

Wesley's Story

My journey with this book mirrors Wesley's own in fascinating ways. In 1725, a young John Wesley picked up *The Imitation of Christ* for the first time. He was preparing for ordination in the Church of England, and a friend had recommended it. At first, Wesley was put off by the book's severity; it seemed to suggest that following Christ meant giving up all earthly happiness. But as he kept reading, something deeper took hold.

"I began to see," Wesley later wrote, "that true religion was seated in the heart, and that God's law extended to all our thoughts as well as words and actions." This insight sparked what Wesley called his "awakening to inward holiness." He began to set aside daily time for prayer and reflection. He examined his *motives*, not just his *actions*. He aimed at—and prayed for—holiness from the inside out.

Ten years later, Wesley published his own edition of *The Imitation of Christ*, which he titled *The Christian's Pattern*. He revised and expanded it in 1741, the edition this adaptation is based on. He wanted to make this medieval spiritual classic accessible to ordinary Christians in 18th-century England. Wesley wasn't just an editor; he was a curator, carefully adapting a Catholic devotional work for Protestant readers, while preserving what he considered its essential spiritual wisdom.

Who Was Thomas à Kempis?

Thomas Hemerken (1380–1471) took his name from his birthplace, the German village of Kempis. Born to humble, pious parents, Thomas was sent at age thirteen to study in Deventer in the Netherlands, which was then a thriving center of learning and spiritual renewal. There, he encountered the *Devotio Moderna* (*Modern Devotion*), a movement emphasizing personal piety, inner spiritual transformation, and the imitation of Christ's life.

At age twenty, Thomas joined the Augustinian monastery at Mount St. Agnes near Zwolle, where his older brother served as prior. For the next seventy-one years, Thomas lived a quiet life of prayer, study, and writing. He spent countless hours copying the Bible by hand and composing devotional works. Around 1441, he completed *The Imitation of Christ*, a work that would become, after the Bible, one of the most widely read Christian books in history.

Those who knew Thomas described him as gentle, patient, and deeply devoted. He seemed to radiate an inner peace that came from long hours in prayer. When he spoke about God and spiritual things, his words "flowed like a stream from an inexhaustible fountain." He died in 1471 at the age of ninety-one, having spent seven decades pursuing the life he wrote about: intimate friendship with Christ and transformation into His likeness.

Why Wesley Treasured This Book

Throughout his long life, Wesley read and reread *The Imitation of Christ* more than any other book except the Bible. He called it a book "next to the Bible" and recommended it constantly to early Methodists. Why did he value it so highly?

First, because it centers on the heart of Christian life: becoming like Christ. Wesley believed that true Christianity wasn't merely about right beliefs or outward religious practices, but about inward transformation. À Kempis captured this perfectly with his focus on humility, self-surrender, trust in God, and loving union with Christ.

Second, because it emphasized what Wesley called "Christian perfection," the possibility of growing in love until our hearts are fully given to God. This wasn't about sinless perfection but being perfected in love. À Kempis showed the path: beginning with humility, moving through self-examination and the slow dying to sin, and culminating in a heart fully united to God's will.

Third, because it was intensely practical. À Kempis didn't write theological treatises; he wrote a guidebook for daily Christian living. How do you handle criticism? How do you deal with your own failures? How do you grow closer to God? These were the questions à Kempis addressed, and Wesley found his answers both biblical and deeply helpful.

Why This Book Matters for Methodists Today

The Wesleyan tradition has always emphasized "practical divinity" or faith that transforms how we actually live. We talk about going on to perfection, about growing in grace, and about holiness of heart and life. But what does that look like day by day? How do we actually grow in Christlikeness?

The Christian's Pattern offers time-tested wisdom for this journey. It addresses the struggles that every serious Christian faces: pride, self-will, impatience, discouragement, spiritual dryness, and the constant pull of competing desires. More importantly, it points the way forward through self-knowledge, surrender to God, daily spiritual practices, and above all, keeping our eyes fixed on Jesus.

This book has shaped Methodist spirituality for nearly three centuries. The Methodist class meeting with its searching questions about the state of one's soul echoes à Kempis' emphasis on self-examination. The Methodist practice of frequent communion finds support in Book Four's teaching on the sacrament as a means of grace. The Methodist pursuit of holiness follows the same path à Kempis laid out: humility, self-renunciation, resignation to God's will, and union with Christ.

About This Edition

This is not a direct translation of the medieval Latin original. Rather, it is a modern paraphrase of Wesley's 1741 edition of *The Christian's Pattern* and that choice of edition matters.

Wesley first published *The Christian's Pattern* in 1735 before his famous Aldersgate experience. In that edition, he made deliberate choices to remove certain chapters from à Kempis' original, shaping the work for a Protestant audience and trimming what he felt was less essential. The 1741 edition restored those chapters. Everything in the 1741 edition is drawn from à Kempis' original book; nothing was added that wasn't already there. Wesley simply gave readers the fuller à Kempis experience, all 88 chapters organized into four books, while retaining his Protestant adaptations. For readers who want the complete breadth of à Kempis' wisdom within Wesley's framework, 1741 is the right edition, and it's the one this adaptation is based on.

Wesley himself worked from an earlier English Protestant translation, revising to improve clarity and accuracy. He also removed or softened some elements of Catholic theology and practice that he felt were unhelpful for Protestant readers, not because he disrespected the Catholic tradition but because he was adapting the work for a different audience. Our goal has been to do the same thing Wesley did: take this timeless material and make it fully accessible to the people who need it most.

We've rendered 18th-century English into contemporary language, similar to how the New Living Translation treats the Bible, clear and readable but reverent and substantial.

We've also added three features to enhance your reading: brief footnotes noting where Wesley made significant adaptations from the original Latin text; a reflection at the end of each chapter connecting its themes to contemporary Christian life; and a prayer to help you respond to what you've read.

This book is meant to be read slowly, prayerfully, and repeatedly. Don't rush through it. Let it work on you. Wesley read it throughout his life, and each time he found new depths. You will too.

How to Use This Book

The following guidance is adapted from John Wesley's original preface to *The Christian's Pattern* (1741), where he offered practical advice for reading spiritual books with profit.

Come with the Right Spirit

The way you approach this book matters as much as the book itself. Here's what will help you benefit most from your reading:

> **Read humbly**. Come as a learner, not a critic. Don't read to evaluate the author's ideas or to find things you disagree with. Read to let God speak to you through these pages. Be willing to be taught, corrected, and changed.
>
> **Read with desire.** Approach this book like a hungry person approaches food or a thirsty person approaches water. Your soul needs spiritual nourishment as much as your body needs physical nourishment. Come with genuine hunger for God and for growth in holiness.
>
> **Read with an honest heart.** Be willing to see yourself as you really are. This book will hold up a mirror to your soul, showing you things you may not want to see, like pride, selfishness, double-mindedness, or lukewarmness. Don't turn away. The first step toward health is accurate diagnosis.
>
> **Read with intention.** Don't read merely to gain knowledge or to feel inspired. Read with the determination to actually practice what you learn. Knowledge that doesn't lead to obedience is worse than no knowledge at all. As you read, ask yourself, "What do I need to do differently because of this?"

How to Read

Read slowly. This isn't a book to race through. Read a chapter (or even just part of a chapter) at a time. Let the words sink in. Pause when something strikes you. Reread sections that challenge or convict you.

Read prayerfully. Begin each reading time by asking God to open your heart and mind. Read with a spirit of conversation with God, pausing to pray about what you're reading. End by asking God to help you live out what you've learned.

Read repeatedly. The richest spiritual books reward multiple readings. You'll notice things the second or third time through that you missed the first time. Different passages will speak to you during different seasons of life. Consider reading through the entire book once a year.

Read with application. As you read, continually ask, "How does this apply to me? What is God saying to me through this? What needs to change in my life?" Write down specific insights and convictions. Share what you're learning with a trusted friend or spiritual mentor.

Read alongside Scripture. This book is full of biblical wisdom, but it's not Scripture itself. Read it in conjunction with daily Bible reading and let the Bible be your ultimate authority. Notice how à Kempis saturates his writing with scriptural language and concepts.

A Pattern for Daily Reading

Prepare (1–2 minutes): Find a quiet place. Take a few deep breaths. Ask God to speak to you through what you're about to read.

Read (5–10 minutes): Read the day's chapter slowly and attentively. When something strikes you, pause and sit with it.

Reflect (5 minutes): Read the reflection at the end of the chapter. Consider the questions it raises. How does this chapter address your current circumstances or struggles?

Pray (3–5 minutes): Use the prayer provided, making it your own. Add your own words. Be specific about how you need God's help to live out what you've read.

Act (Throughout the day): Choose one concrete thing from your reading to practice that day. Return to it mentally during the day. Ask God for grace to follow through.

Don't Read This Book If...

Let's be honest: This book isn't for everyone. Or rather, it's not for everyone in every season. Don't read this book if:

You're looking for light, easy inspiration. This book requires serious engagement and self-examination.

You're not willing to be challenged. À Kempis pulls no punches about the cost of discipleship.

You're in a season of severe doubt or spiritual crisis. Get more foundational help first; come back to this later.

You're dealing with clinical depression or overwhelming guilt. This book's call to self-examination could be harmful rather than helpful in that state. Get professional support first.

This book is for those who want to go deeper with God, who are willing to face uncomfortable truths about themselves, and who are ready to pursue holiness with seriousness and joy.

A Word of Encouragement

If you're just beginning your journey of intentional discipleship, some of what you read here may seem overwhelming. That's okay. Don't let it discourage you. À Kempis is describing the mature Christian life as a goal to grow toward, not a standard to meet immediately.

God meets you where you are. He doesn't demand instant perfection, but He does invite steady progress. Take what speaks to you now. Come back later for what doesn't yet make sense. And remember, this entire book is about imitating Christ, who is "gentle and lowly in heart" (Matthew 11:29). He walks with you on this journey.

The goal is not to master this book but to let it help you grow in knowing and loving Jesus Christ. As you read, pray Wesley's own prayer: "Lord, increase my faith; confirm my hope; perfect me in love."

My Hope for You

When I first encountered *The Imitation of Christ* as a young man, I was hungry for God in a way I couldn't fully articulate. The book met me in that hunger. Now, over three decades into pastoral ministry, I find myself hungry again but differently. I'm hungry for depth in a shallow age. For quiet in a noisy world. For transformation in a culture of constant distraction.

I suspect you may be hungry too. Maybe, like me, you've had fits and starts in your devotional life. Maybe you know you need something more but aren't sure where to find it. Maybe you picked up this book because you're tired of spiritual junk food and you're ready for a feast.

If so, you're in the right place. This book has nourished Christians for six hundred years. It shaped John Wesley and through him, the Methodist movement. It can shape you too, not by adding more religious activity to your life, but by helping you become the person God created you to be.

My prayer is that this modern paraphrase will bless you as we press on toward becoming fully formed followers of Jesus. May the same God who met Wesley and who met me in these pages, meet you here as well.

Let's begin.

Keys for Reading

Each daily reading is divided into four sections.

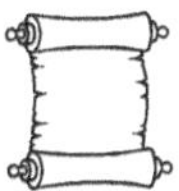

Original source material paraphrased for modern readers

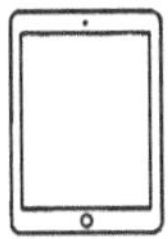

Author's Reflection

Action steps to walk it out and bring the wisdom in the pages to life

A prayer to breathe its wisdom into your life

THE CHRISTIAN'S PATTERN – BOOK ONE

THE SPIRITUAL LIFE

1

Following Jesus, Not the World

He that followeth me, walketh not in darkness, saith the Lord These are the words of Christ, by which we are admonished, how we ought to imitate his life and manners.

—The Christian's Pattern, 1741

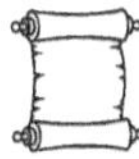

1. "Whoever follows me will never walk in darkness, but will have the light of life" (John 8:12). These are Jesus' own words, calling us to imitate His life and character if we want to be truly enlightened and freed from spiritual blindness. Let our highest priority, then, be to reflect deeply on the life of Jesus Christ.
2. What good does it do to argue brilliantly about the Trinity if you lack humility and end up offending the very God you're discussing? The truth is that impressive words don't make you holy or righteous; a godly life makes you dear to God. I'd rather experience genuine sorrow for my sins than merely understand the theological definition of repentance. Even if you memorized the entire Bible and could quote every philosopher who ever lived, what would it profit you without love for God (1 Corinthians 13:2)? It's all meaningless; everything is meaningless except loving God and serving Him alone (Ecclesiastes 1:2).
3. So, it's meaningless to chase after wealth that won't last. It's meaningless to crave recognition and status. It's meaningless to indulge every physical desire, especially when it leads to consequences you'll regret. It's meaningless to wish for a long life while caring nothing about living well. It's meaningless to focus on this present world while ignor-

ing what comes after. It's meaningless to set your heart on things that quickly fade away instead of hurrying toward the place where joy lasts forever.

Here's what strikes me about this opening chapter: À Kempis doesn't ease us in gently. He goes straight for the jugular. *What is your life really about?* Not what you say it's about but what your actual choices reveal it's about?

I think about my own journey here. When I first read this in my twenties, I was the person described here: deeply religious, eager to learn, ready to debate theology. I knew my doctrines. I could argue fine points of Scripture. But when à Kempis asked, "What would it profit you without love for God?" I had to admit that my heart was often cold. I was more in love with being right than with being loving and more impressed with my knowledge than concerned about my character.

The diagnostic test is beautifully simple: Does your faith produce increasing love for God and others, or is it just correct beliefs and religious activity? Because here's the thing, you can have all the right answers and still completely miss the point.

The list of "vanities" in passage 3 reads like he's been scrolling through our Instagram feeds. Chasing wealth? Check. Craving status and recognition? Double check. Even many sincere Christians operate with what I call "practical atheism," believing in heaven theoretically but living for earth exclusively.

So, here's the uncomfortable question: If someone examined your calendar and bank account this past month—no explanations allowed, just the raw data—what would they conclude you're living for?

Try this: Look at your calendar. Move one thing this week to make room for what you actually say you believe.

Lord Jesus, you promised that whoever follows you will not walk in darkness. I confess I've been content with knowing about you rather than truly knowing you and with right beliefs but a cold heart. Forgive me for pursuing empty things while neglecting what is eternal. Give me a heart that loves you, not just a mind that understands theology. Help me meditate on your life and let your character be formed in me. Show me where I've been chasing vanity—wealth, status, pleasure, approval. Reorder my love so that loving and serving you becomes my chief endeavor. Shine your light into every corner of my heart. Deliver me from spiritual blindness. Make me truly yours. Amen.

2
Thinking Humbly of Ourselves

All men naturally desire to know; but what availeth knowledge, without the fear of God? Better of a surety is a lowly peasant who serveth God, than a proud philosopher who watcheth the stars and neglecteth the knowledge of himself.

—The Christian's Pattern, 1741

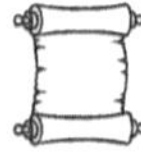

1. Everyone naturally wants to know things, but what good is knowledge without reverence for God? A humble farmer who serves God faithfully is better than a brilliant philosopher who neglects his own soul while studying the stars. Those who truly know themselves see their own sinfulness and aren't impressed by human praise. Even if I understood everything in the world, if I lacked love, how would that help me before God, who judges by actions not knowledge (1 Corinthians 13:2–3)?

2. Stop obsessing over knowing more and more; that path leads to distraction and self-deception. There are many things that, knowing them, do little to benefit your soul. It's foolish to focus on anything other than what genuinely matters for your spiritual wellbeing. Lots of words don't satisfy the soul, but a clear conscience gives you confidence before God.

3. The more you know and the better you understand, the more strictly you'll be judged unless your life becomes correspondingly holier (Luke 12:48). So don't get puffed up with knowledge. Instead, let what you know make you

more aware of your accountability. If you think you know a lot, remember there's infinitely more you don't know.

4. The highest and most valuable lesson you can learn is true self-knowledge. Real wisdom means thinking nothing of yourself and always thinking well of others. Even if you see someone else sin publicly, don't consider yourself naturally superior to them. We're all frail and prone to failure, so remember, you're no exception.

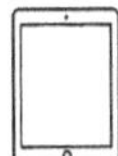

Let me be honest, humility might be the most countercultural virtue in our age. We live in a culture obsessed with self-promotion, personal branding, and showcasing expertise. Social media has turned everyone into their own PR firm.

But here's what à Kempis is actually saying and what this quote captures perfectly: "Humility is not thinking less of yourself, it's thinking of yourself less."[1] There's a world of difference.

The warning in passage 3 keeps me up at night: "The more you know and the better you understand, the more strictly you'll be judged unless your life becomes more holy." Think about that. Education, theological training, biblical knowledge, all of it increases responsibility. It should make us more aware of how much we fall short, not more confident in our superiority.

Here's my diagnostic test: Does your spiritual knowledge make you more humble or more proud? More patient with others' failures or more judgmental? Knowledge that doesn't transform character isn't wisdom. It's just trivia.

Try this: Pick one thing you know but haven't practiced yet. Do it today, just that one thing.

---

1. Warren, Rick. *The Purpose Driven Life: What on Earth Am I Here For?* Zondervan, 2013.

Lord, I confess that I often value being smart more than being humble. I want to be recognized, celebrated, and seen as knowledgeable and capable. Forgive my pride. Teach me true self-knowledge, to see myself honestly without either pride or despair. Help me understand that all my knowledge means nothing if I don't grow in love and holiness. Keep me from using spiritual language to impress others while my heart remains cold. Give me a pure conscience before you, not an impressive reputation before people. Make me truly humble, not with false modesty but with honest awareness of who I am and who you are. Amen.

3

Living in Truth

Happy is he, whom Truth itself teacheth, not by figures and words that pass away; but as Truth is. Our own opinion and our own senses do often deceive us and discern but little.

—The Christian's Pattern, 1741

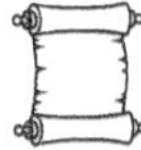

1. Blessed is the person whom truth itself teaches, not through symbols and passing words, but through direct, personal encounter. Our own opinions and assumptions often deceive us, and we see very little clearly. What's the point of debating obscure theological questions that won't even come up on judgment day? It's utterly foolish to neglect what's truly profitable while chasing curious or harmful knowledge.
2. The person to whom the eternal Word speaks directly is freed from a thousand pointless opinions. From this one Word comes all things, and all things point back to Him (John 1:1–3). No one truly understands or judges rightly without Him. God, you who are Truth itself (John 14:6), make me one with you in everlasting love. I'm weary of reading and hearing so many things; in you alone is everything I desire (Psalm 73:25).
3. The simpler a person's heart is, the more they understand without effort because they receive the light of knowledge from above (James 1:5). A pure, simple, and stable spirit isn't scattered even when busy with many tasks because everything is done for God's glory, not for selfish gain. This

should be our daily work: conquering ourselves and making steady progress in holiness.

4. Every form of perfection in this life has some imperfection mixed into it (1 Corinthians 13:12). Humble self-knowledge is a surer path to God than the deepest scholarship.
5. If people worked as hard at rooting out their sins as they do at debating theological questions, there would be far less evil in the world! On judgment day, we won't be examined on what we read but on what we did, not on how eloquently we spoke but on how faithfully we lived (Matthew 25:31–46).
6. True greatness belongs to those who are great in love (1 Corinthians 13:13). True greatness belongs to those who think little of themselves and care nothing for worldly honors. True wisdom belongs to those who count everything else as garbage compared to knowing Christ (Philippians 3:8). And true learning belongs to those who do God's will and surrender their own.

À Kempis draws a stark contrast between two ways of knowing: head knowledge that puffs up and heart knowledge that transforms. He's not anti-intellectual; he's anti-intellectualism-without-transformation.

We can become experts on theology, biblical languages, and church history and still have cold, unchanged hearts. Meanwhile, simple believers who encounter "Truth itself" in personal communion with God often display more wisdom than scholars. I've seen people in my own congregation with eighth-grade educations who know Jesus intimately, whose lives radiate His character, who pray with power, and who love with abandon.

Wesley himself warned about this very danger. In a 1768 letter to Joseph Benson, he wrote, "Beware that you be not swallowed up in books! An ounce of love is worth a pound of knowledge."

Here's the self-examination: When you read Scripture or spiritual books, are you primarily gathering information or genuinely listening for God's voice? Does your growing knowledge produce growing humility and love or just more confidence in your own opinions? Are you becoming more like Jesus or just more informed about Jesus?

Try this: Before your next spiritual conversation, ask yourself, Am I trying to impress or am I trying to grow?

God, you are Truth itself. I confess I'm often satisfied with secondhand knowledge about you rather than direct encounters with you. I collect information, master concepts, and form opinions, but my heart remains unchanged. Forgive me. I'm weary of mere words and ideas. Teach me yourself. Speak directly to my heart. Make me simple enough to hear you, pure enough to see you, and stable enough to rest in you. Show me where I'm pursuing recognition and worldly greatness instead of humble obedience. Unite all my scattered desires in love for you alone. Give me a heart that's great in love, little in its own eyes, and surrendered completely to your will. Amen.

4

Wise Choices

We ought not to give credit to every word and suggestion; but to consider cautiously and patiently, what things are according to the will of God.

—The Christian's Pattern, 1741

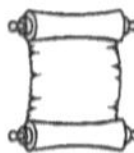

1. We shouldn't believe every rumor or react to every suggestion. Instead, we should carefully and prayerfully consider things according to God's will. But sadly, our human weakness makes us more likely to believe and repeat negative things about others than positive things. Wise people don't automatically believe everything they hear because they know how prone human nature is to evil and how easily we fail in our words (James 3:2).
2. True wisdom means not being rash in your actions and not stubbornly clinging to your own opinions. Wisdom means not believing everything you hear and not immediately passing along to others what you've heard or think you believe. Seek counsel from someone wise and conscientious. Be willing to learn from someone better than yourself rather than always following your own ideas (Proverbs 12:15). A godly life makes you wise in God's eyes and gives you experience in many things. The more humble you are and the more surrendered to God, the more prudent and content you'll be in everything.

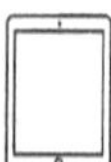

À Kempis addresses what might be the most needed virtue in our social media age: wisdom in speech and judgment. We live in a culture of hot takes, instant reactions, viral rumors, and cancel culture where everyone has an opinion about everything and feels compelled to share it immediately.

This chapter offers ancient wisdom for our moment: slow down, verify before you spread information, resist the urge to believe and repeat the worst about others, seek wise counsel before acting, and hold your own opinions loosely.

And boy, do I need this one. My wife often (rightly) reminds me of how "pig-headed" I can be when it comes to my opinions. I can dig in, convinced I'm right and unwilling to listen to other perspectives.

The antidote to rashness and gossip? Humility and surrender to God. The humbler one is, and more resigned unto God, the more prudent and contented we will be in all things. When you're secure in God rather than in being right, you can afford to be patient, discerning, and gracious.

Try this: Identify one decision you've been overthinking. Bring it to God before you bring it to anyone else.

Lord, forgive me for being quick to believe and repeat negative things about others. Forgive my rashness in judgment, my stubbornness in my own opinions, and my eagerness to pass along gossip or unverified information. Give me wisdom to slow down, to verify before I speak, and to seek wise counsel before I act. Help me hold my opinions loosely and be willing to learn from others. Make me humble enough to be prudent and surrendered enough to be content. Guard my tongue from speaking evil. In a world of hot takes and instant reactions, teach me the wisdom of patience, discernment, and grace. Amen.

5

Reading Scripture

In reading of Holy Scripture, truth is to be looked for, rather than eloquence. And all Scripture is to be read with the same spirit wherewith it was written.

—The Christian's Pattern, 1741

1. When you read Holy Scripture, seek truth, not eloquence. All Scripture should be read in the same Spirit that inspired it (2 Timothy 3:16). Be as willing to read simple, devotional books as you are to read complex, scholarly ones. Don't let the reputation of the author, whether famous or obscure, determine what you read. Let your love of pure truth be your guide. Don't focus on who said something; focus on what was said.
2. People come and go, but the truth of the Lord remains forever (Psalm 119:89). God speaks to us in many different ways without playing favorites. Our own curiosity often gets in the way when we read Scripture; we want to analyze and debate things we should simply accept and obey. If you want to benefit from reading, approach it humbly, simply, and faithfully. Ask questions willingly and listen in silence to the wisdom of godly people.

À Kempis offers a radically different approach to Bible reading than what dominates much of contemporary Christianity. We live in an age of Bible studies, commentaries, theological debates, and endless analysis. None of that is wrong, but à Kempis warns that curiosity and intellectual inquiry can actually hinder us if they become the primary way we engage Scripture.

Here's where I have to confess something personal. I know from Gary Thomas' book *Sacred Pathways* that I'm wired as an "intellectual;" I naturally connect with God through study, through ideas, and through understanding.[2] The danger for people like me is exactly what à Kempis warns about here: I can collect insights about God instead of encountering God Himself.

The key phrase is this: "All Scripture should be read by the same spirit wherewith it was written," the Holy Spirit. You can study the Bible for years and miss God entirely if you approach it merely as an intellectual exercise rather than as a personal encounter with the living God. The goal isn't to master Scripture but to let Scripture master you.

Dallas Willard was known to say, "Bible study without obedience is just daydreaming about transformation." Ouch.

Try this: Pick one verse today. Don't study it; sit with it. Let it read you.

Lord, forgive me for the times I've approached your Word with more curiosity than hunger and more analysis than obedience. I've studied to impress others or win arguments rather than to know you and be transformed by you. Teach me to read Scripture in the same Spirit that inspired it. Give me a humble heart that comes to learn, not to judge. Give me a simple heart that seeks your truth, not eloquence or cleverness. Give me a faithful heart that responds in obedience to what I read. Help me stop debating things I should simply accept and obey. Speak to me through your Word today. Transform me by the truth I encounter. Amen.

2. Thomas, Gary. *Sacred Pathways: Nine Ways to Connect with God.* Zondervan, 2020.

6

Avoiding Pride and False Hope

Vain is the man who putteth his trust in men, or in any created thing. Be not ashamed to serve others for the love of Jesus Christ, and to be esteemed poor in this world.

—The Christian's Pattern, 1741

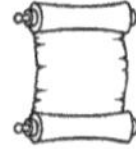

1. It's foolish to put your trust in people or created things (Psalm 146:3). Don't be ashamed to serve others for the love of Jesus Christ or to be considered unimpressive by the world's standards. Don't presume on your own abilities; put your trust in God. Do what you can, and God will support your good intentions. Don't trust in your knowledge or in any other person; trust in the grace of God, who helps the humble and humbles the proud (James 4:6).
2. Don't take pride in your wealth or your influential friends; take pride in God, who gives all things and desires to give you Himself above all (1 Corinthians 1:31). Don't value yourself based on your physical strength or appearance, for a minor illness can destroy both. Don't take pride in your natural talents or intelligence because that displeases God.
3. Don't consider yourself better than others, or God may judge you worse than them (Luke 18:9–14). Don't be proud of your good works because God's judgment is completely different from human judgment. If there's anything good in you, believe that there's even more good in others. It doesn't hurt you to think of yourself as the worst of all people, but it does hurt you to consider yourself better than anyone else (1 Timothy 1:15). The humble enjoy continual peace, but the proud heart is full of envy and constant irritation.

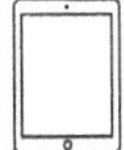

À Kempis systematically dismantles every foundation we typically build our identity on, including knowledge, appearance, talent, achievements, wealth, connections, and even our good works. None of these are reliable grounds for confidence because they're all temporary and all subject to God's judgment.

This hits our achievement obsessed, image curating, comparison driven culture right between the eyes. Social media has weaponized comparison and turned it into FOMO. We scroll through everyone else's highlight reel and feel like we're falling behind.

À Kempis offers a radical alternative: "If there is any good in you, believe that there is much more in others." This stance protects you from the poison of pride and produces peace. "The humble enjoy continued peace, but in the heart of the proud is envy and frequent indignation." Pride makes you perpetually anxious about your standing. Humility sets you free from all that exhausting nonsense.

Try this: Notice the next moment you're performing for approval. Stop. Pray instead. Nobody needs to know.

Lord, I confess I've built my identity on the shifting sand of my abilities, my achievements, and my reputation. I compare myself to others constantly and find no peace. Forgive my pride. Teach me to place my trust in you alone. Help me see that any good in me is your gift, and there's likely more good in others than I recognize. Free me from the exhausting work of self-promotion and comparison. Give me true humility, not self-hatred but an honest assessment that looks to you for worth. Replace the envy and irritation of pride with the peace that comes from resting in you. Amen.

7

Healthy Boundaries

Open not thine heart to everyone but treat of thy affairs with a man that is wise and that feareth God.

—The Christian's Pattern, 1741

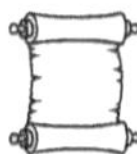

Don't open your heart to just anyone. Instead, discuss your personal matters with wise people who fear God (Proverbs 13:20). Don't spend too much time with young people and strangers. Don't flatter wealthy people, and don't go out of your way to appear before influential people. Instead, keep company with humble and simple people and with those who are devout and virtuous. Talk with them about things that build you up spiritually (1 Corinthians 15:33). Don't be overly familiar with anyone but commend all good people to God. Desire to be intimate with God alone and with His angels and avoid seeking recognition from people. We must have love for everyone, but close familiarity with everyone is neither wise nor helpful (Psalm 1:1).[3]

À Kempis is addressing something we desperately need to hear in our oversharing culture: Not everyone deserves access to your inner life. We live in a world where people broadcast their deepest struggles to strangers on social media, where "authenticity" has become performative.

But notice carefully, the chapter isn't promoting isolation or elitism. He says explicitly: "we must show love to everyone." Love ev-

3. The 1741 edition does not include numbering. This section was left to match the format of the original source material.

eryone. Show kindness to everyone. Treat everyone with dignity and respect. But be selective about intimacy. There's a huge difference between Christian love (which extends to all) and close friendship (which requires discernment).

The warning against flattering the rich and courting influential people cuts against our networking culture where we're taught to build our brand and make connections. À Kempis says seek out humble, simple, and devout people instead, those who will help you grow spiritually, not advance your career.

The core principle is "Seek intimacy with God and His angels alone and avoid seeking approval from people." Your deepest intimacy should be with God. Human relationships, even good ones, can become substitutes for that primary relationship if we're not careful.

Try this: Name one relationship where you're seeking what only God can give. Bring that need to him today.

Lord, forgive me for being careless with my heart, opening it to anyone and everyone, seeking intimacy in the wrong places, and oversharing with people who can't or shouldn't carry the weight of my inner life. Give me wisdom to know who I should confide in and who I should keep at a healthy distance. Guard me from the temptation to flatter the powerful or seek recognition from influential people. Instead, draw me to the humble, simple, devout people who will help me grow spiritually. Most of all, teach me to desire intimacy with you above all else. Help me order my relationships rightly, loving all but reserving my inmost heart for you alone. Amen.

8
Taming Our Desires

Flee the tumult of the world as much as thou canst; for the treating of worldly affairs doth very much hinder, though they be done with a sincere intention.

—*The Christian's Pattern, 1741*

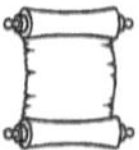

1. Avoid the chaos and noise of the world as much as you can, because we're quickly defiled and distracted by empty talk (Proverbs 10:19). I wish I had kept silent more often and hadn't spent so much time in company. Why are we so eager to talk when we rarely return to silence without some damage to our conscience? We willingly talk about what we love most or what troubles us most (Luke 6:45), but sadly, it's often pointless and leads nowhere. This outward comfort actually blocks deeper, inward peace with God. Therefore, we must watch and pray so our time doesn't slip away uselessly (Matthew 26:41).
2. When it's appropriate and helpful to speak, say things that build others up (Ephesians 4:29). Genuine spiritual conversation, especially among people who share the same mind and spirit in God, greatly helps our spiritual growth.

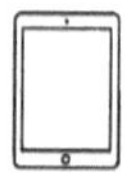

À Kempis addresses what might be the most challenging spiritual discipline for modern people: silence. We live in the noisiest age in human history. Constant notifications. Endless content. 24/7 news. Podcasts. Music. Social media. We've lost the capacity for silence and solitude.

I confess this is one of my biggest struggles. My default is noise. When I'm cooking, the podcast is playing. When I'm driving, the audiobook is on. When I'm working, the music is streaming. Silence feels... uncomfortable. Empty. Wasteful, even.

The insight that "we readily talk about what we love or desire most or about what troubles and frustrates us" is profound. Our speech reveals what dominates our hearts. The warning that "outward comfort blocks inward consolation" is crucial. We seek comfort in conversation, in being heard and understood. But we talk to everyone else before we talk to God, and we wonder why we lack peace.

Think about how often we do this; something happens, good or bad, and our immediate impulse is to text someone, call someone, or post about it. What if our first impulse was to bring it to God in prayer instead?

Try this: The next time something happens today, good or bad, pray before you text, post, or call.

Lord, I confess I fill my life with noise, constant talk, endless consumption of words, and very little silence. I process everything by talking about it rather than by bringing it to you first in prayer. Forgive me for seeking comfort in conversation more than in communion with you. Forgive me for wasting time in empty talk that damages my conscience and clutters my soul. Teach me the discipline of silence. Help me watch and pray rather than letting time slip away uselessly. When I do speak, let my words build others up and point toward you. Guard my tongue from useless chatter. Guard my heart from the constant need to be heard, understood, and validated by others. Let me find my deepest consolation in you, not in outward comfort. Amen.

9

Finding Peace and Growing Spiritually

We might enjoy much peace, if we would not busy ourselves with the words and deeds of others, and things which appertain not to our charge.

—The Christian's Pattern, 1741

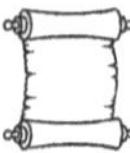

1. We'd have a lot more peace if we stopped poking around in other people's business, their words, choices, and drama. None of it is ours to carry. How does anyone stay at peace when they're constantly in everyone else's affairs and never once look at their own? The people who find real peace are the ones who stay focused (Matthew 5:8).
2. We're too tangled up in our own cravings and too anxious about things that won't last. There's no real hunger to grow, and so we stay flat and cold, just going through the motions.
3. If we were truly done with ourselves and had stopped chasing what the world offers, we'd start experiencing something of God. But the moment things get hard, we run straight to people instead of to Him.
4. If we'd actually show up for the fight and dig in like people who are serious about it, we'd feel God's strength behind us (Ephesians 6:10–13). He puts us in the battle because He knows we can win it. But we have to go after the root, not just the surface (Matthew 3:10). Deal with the desires that are pulling you off course; cut them out at the source. That's when the soul finally gets to rest.

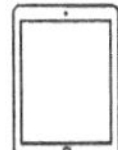

Here's what keeps me up at night about this chapter: the accusation that I'm spiritually cold and indifferent. Because the thing is, I can look busy. I can have a full calendar of church activities, ministry responsibilities, and Bible studies. I can look very spiritual. But à Kempis asks the piercing question, Am I actually inflamed with fervent desire to grow better every day? Or am I just going through the motions?

The first passage hits hard too: "We might enjoy much peace, if we would not busy ourselves with the words and deeds of others." How much of my emotional energy gets spent tracking what other people are doing, saying, believing, and posting?

Social media has turned us all into amateur surveillance agents. We monitor everyone else's lives, offering unsolicited commentary, and keeping score of who's right and who's wrong. Meanwhile, we rarely examine our own hearts with the same scrutiny we apply to everyone else.

The final passage offers both challenge and hope; "Let us lay the axe to the root," not just pruning surface behaviors but getting at the disordered passions underneath and not just managing symptoms but attacking the disease. This is hard, slow work. But he promises that "being freed from passions, we may find rest to our souls."

Try this: Name the one thing stealing your peace right now. Hand it to God by name, out loud.

Lord, forgive me for being spiritually cold while looking busy and religious. Forgive me for turning to human comfort first instead of running to you. Kindle in me a fervent desire to grow spiritually better every day. Make me single-hearted andfocused on you alone, not pulled in a dozen directions by things that are none of my concern. Give me courage to stand firm in spiritual battle. Help me lay the axe to the root of my disordered passions, not just managing symptoms but getting at the disease underneath. Teach me to find my rest in you alone. Amen.

10

The Gift of Hard Times

It is good for us that we sometimes have sorrows and adversities; for they make a man enter into himself, that he may know that he is an exile here, and may not place his trust in any worldly thing.

—The Christian's Pattern, 1741

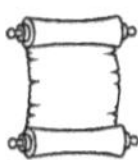

1. It's actually good for us to have troubles and difficulties sometimes; they push us inward and stop us from trusting the world. It's good to be contradicted, to have people misjudge us even when our motives are right. Those experiences drive us to God as our true witness, especially when we're being judged unfairly by others (Romans 8:16).
2. So, a person needs to be so deeply rooted in God that they don't need to go looking for comfort from people. When you're hurting, tempted, or fighting dark thoughts, you quickly realize just how much you need God.
3. As long as we're in this world, temptation is part of the deal (Job 7:1). Stay on top of your own struggles and keep praying; don't give the enemy a foothold (1 Peter 5:8).
4. Temptations are often more useful than they are comfortable; they humble us, purify us, and teach us things we couldn't learn any other way.
5. Nobody gets through life without being tempted. One leaves and another shows up. A lot of people try to run from temptation and end up deeper in it. Running doesn't work. Patience and genuine humility are what defeat our spiritual enemies.
6. Dealing with temptation on the surface without pulling it out at the root doesn't get you anywhere. It just comes

back. Slow and steady (with patience and God's help) beats hard effort in your own strength every time. When you're being tempted, get counsel. And go easy on others who are struggling.

7. Temptation starts with a restless, unanchored mind and not enough trust in God. Fire tests iron; temptation tests the righteous (1 Peter 1:7). What you do when you're tempted reveals who you actually are. Catch it early; the enemy is far easier to deal with at the door than once he's inside. It starts with a thought. Then, imagination runs with it. Then, it starts to feel appealing. Then, you say yes (James 1:15).
8. Some people face their hardest temptations early in their faith and others near the end. Some fight them most of their lives. Some barely at all. God in His wisdom knows exactly what each person can bear, and He orders all of it toward the salvation of His people.
9. When temptation hits hard, pray harder. God will always provide a way through (1 Corinthians 10:13). Humble yourself under His hand in every trial; He lifts up the humble (1 Peter 5:6).
10. Temptation and trouble are where you find out how far you've actually come. Anybody can be devoted when life is easy. But the person who holds on patiently through real hardship is someone going somewhere. Some people who survive the big temptations get tripped up by small ones, which is exactly the point. They will stop trusting themselves, having seen how fragile they really are.

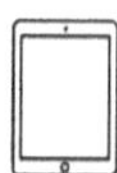

If I'm honest, my default response to adversity is "Get me out of here." My prayers during hard times sound less like "Lord, what are you teaching me?" and more like "Lord, make it stop!"

But à Kempis flips the script; troubles are actually good because they force us to look inward and stop trusting worldly things. They reveal what we're actually made of.

The progression of temptation in passage 7 is worth memorizing:

simple evil thought → strong imagination →
delight → consent

The enemy doesn't need us to leap into sin; he just needs us to entertain the thought for a moment.

Here's what I need to hear most: we can't overcome temptation by running from it, only by patience and humility. I can delete apps, change locations, and avoid people, but if I haven't dealt with the root, I'm just playing whack-a-mole.

Try this: Name the temptation you keep running from. Ask God for grace to face it instead of fleeing it.

Lord, I confess my default response to adversity is escape, not growth. I want comfort more than character. Thank you that you're wiser than I am and that you use troubles and temptations to drive me deeper into dependence on you. Help me stop running and start learning. Show me the temptations I'm most vulnerable to. Help me resist at the very beginning, not after I've already compromised. Give me humility to admit I need help and patience to endure through your strength, not mine. When adversity comes, help me ask "What are you teaching me?" instead of "When will this end?" Amen.

11

Don't Judge Too Quickly

Turn thine eyes upon thyself and see that thou judge not the doings of others. In judging others, a man laboreth in vain, often erreth, and easily sinneth; but in judging and examining himself, he always laboreth fruitfully.

—*The Christian's Pattern, 1741*

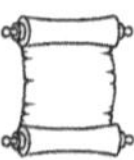

1. Turn your eyes toward yourself and be careful not to judge others' actions (Matthew 7:1–5). In judging others, we labor in vain, often make mistakes, and easily sin. But in judging and examining ourselves, we always labor fruitfully. We often judge things according to our biases; our personal preferences rob us of sound judgment. If God were always our true desire, we wouldn't be so troubled when our preferences are opposed.

2. But often something lurks within us that pulls us toward it. Many people secretly seek their own interests in their actions but don't realize it. They seem to live peacefully when things go according to their will, but if things turn out differently than they want, they're immediately troubled. Different opinions and inclinations often cause conflicts between religious people, between friends, and between fellow countrymen.

3. Old habits die hard, and no one wants to be led farther than they can see for themselves. If you rely more on your own reasoning than on Jesus Christ, you'll be slow (if ever) to become truly enlightened (Proverbs 3:5–6).

This chapter hits me right in the gut every time I read it. "In judging others, we work in vain, often make mistakes, and easily sin." Ouch. I'm a pastor. You know what that means? I spend a lot of time observing people, their choices, their priorities, and their spiritual lives. And it's way too easy to slip from pastoral concern into judgmental criticism.

À Kempis nails the problem; "We often judge things based on our personal preferences because our emotions easily rob us of right judgment." I don't judge objectively. I judge based on my preferences, my personality, my background, and my biases.

Here's the uncomfortable truth: when I'm busy judging everyone else, I'm usually avoiding self-examination. It's easier to see the speck in my brother's eye than the log in my own (Matthew 7:3–5). Judging others is "working in vain," a waste of energy that produces nothing good. But self-examination? That's always fruitful.

Wesley understood this temptation well. He wrote, "I have often repented of judging too severely, but seldom of being too merciful." That's the wisdom we need. When in doubt, err on the side of grace. Assume the best. Give people the benefit of the doubt.

Try this: Think of one person you've been quietly judging. Pray for them by name today and mean it.

Lord Jesus, forgive me for how quickly I judge others while excusing myself. My judgments are tainted by my preferences, my biases, and my need to feel superior. Teach me to turn my eyes toward myself first. Help me examine my own heart with the same scrutiny I apply to everyone else. Show me where I'm secretly seeking my own interests while pretending to serve you. Give me compassion instead of criticism, mercy instead of judgment. When my inclinations are opposed, let that reveal that you're not yet my ultimate desire. Change my heart so that loving and serving you matters more than having things my way. Amen.

12

Love as Your Motive

The outward work without charity profiteth nothing; but whatsoever is done out of charity, be it ever so little and contemptible, is wholly fruitful.

—The Christian's Pattern, 1741

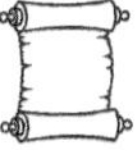

1. Outward work without love accomplishes nothing. But whatever is done out of genuine love, no matter how small or insignificant, is completely fruitful and valuable to God (1 Corinthians 13:1–3). God cares more about how much love motivates our actions than about how much we accomplish. Those who love much accomplish much. Those who do things well accomplish much. And those who serve their neighbor's good rather than their own will do things well.
2. Often what appears to be love is actually just natural inclination: self-interest, self-will, hope of reward, or desire for personal benefit masquerading as charity. These mixed motives are things we're rarely entirely free from.
3. Those who have true and perfect charity seek their own interests in nothing but only desire that God would be glorified in all things (Philippians 2:3–4). They envy no one because they're not seeking personal satisfaction. They attribute nothing good to any person as if it originated there but recognize that all good comes from God, the fountain from which everything flows and in whom all the saints finally find their rest (James 1:17). Oh, if someone had even one spark of true charity, they would immediately see that all earthly things are full of emptiness!

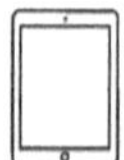

This chapter makes me squirm. Not because I disagree with it but because it exposes how often my motives are mixed, even when I'm doing ministry. "God weighs more with how much love one works, than how much he does." That's both liberating and terrifying. Liberating because it means God values the small act done with great love more than the impressive act done with mixed motives.

How often have I done the right thing for the wrong reason? Did I visit someone in the hospital because I genuinely cared or because it's what good pastors are supposed to do? Or did I preach a sermon to glorify God or to get positive feedback? À Kempis says, "Often it seems to be charity, and it is rather carnality." Ouch.

When I get stuck in that paralyzing self-examination, I'm reminded of the wise words of Bishop Dick Wills, who has told me more than once, "God honors obedience." That's profound. I can't always untangle my motives. I can't manufacture pure love on demand. But I can obey. And God honors that obedience, working through it to purify my heart over time.

As Charles Wesley prayed in one of his hymns, "O for a heart to praise my God, a heart from sin set free, a heart that always feels Your blood so freely shed for me!"[4]

Try this: Choose one act of love today that you don't feel like doing. Do it anyway. Don't mention it.

4. Wesley, Charles, "O for a Heart to Praise My God," in Hymns and Sacred Poems (Bristol: Felix Farley, 1742).

Lord, forgive me for how often my service is tainted with mixed motives. I want credit and recognition, even when I'm supposedly serving you. Expose the self-interest lurking beneath my good deeds. Kindle in me true charity—love that seeks nothing for itself and wants only your glory. Show me where I'm pursuing my own satisfaction under the guise of serving you. Help me see that all my accomplishments mean nothing without love. Teach me to care more about loving well than doing much and more about your approval than human applause. Let genuine love for you and others be the driving force behind everything I do. Amen.

13

Patience with Difficult People

What thou art not able to amend in thyself or in others,
thou oughtest patiently to bear, until God ordain otherwise.

—*The Christian's Pattern, 1741*

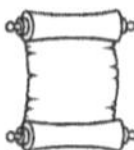

1. Whatever you cannot change in yourself or others, you should bear patiently until God decides to change things. Perhaps this is better for developing your patience.
2. If someone who's been warned once or twice won't change, don't argue with them. Instead, commit everything to God so that His will may be done and His name honored in all His servants, for God knows how to turn evil into good (Romans 8:28). Study to be patient in bearing with others' defects and weaknesses, whatever they may be. Remember, you also have many faults that others must put up with. If you can't make yourself everything you'd like to be, how can you expect to have other people conform perfectly to your preferences? We'd gladly have others be perfect, yet we don't amend our own faults.
3. If everyone were perfect, what would we have to suffer from our neighbor for God's sake? But God has ordained things this way so that we may learn to bear one another's burdens (Galatians 6:2). No one is without fault. No one is self-sufficient. No one has enough wisdom for themselves alone. We must bear with one another, comfort one another, help one another, instruct one another, and admonish one another. Occasions of adversity best reveal how much virtue each person truly has. For challenges don't make a person frail; they simply show what they already are (Luke 6:45).

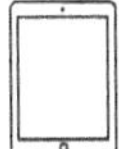

This chapter is a gut-check on how we treat difficult people. Here's the uncomfortable truth: I'm quick to spot everyone else's flaws while making excuses for my own.

À Kempis exposes this double standard brilliantly; "We would willingly have others perfect, and yet we amend not our own faults." We want everyone else strictly corrected while resisting correction ourselves. The line that convicts me most is "If you cannot make yourself into the person you'd like to be, how can you expect to have someone else be exactly to your liking?"

But here's where it gets really good; "If all men were perfect, what should we have to suffer of our neighbor for God?" God deliberately puts imperfect people in our lives, difficult people, annoying people, and people who push our buttons, so we have opportunities to grow in patience, love, and grace. The brilliant insight at the end says, "Occasions of adversity best discover how great virtue each one has." That difficult person in your life? They're not making you impatient; they're revealing the impatience that was already there.

As Jesus said, "Out of the abundance of the heart the mouth speaks" (Luke 6:45). Difficult people are like a stress test for the heart, revealing what's really inside.

Try this: Name the person who irritates you most.
Ask God what that irritation reveals about you.

Lord, forgive me for how harshly I judge others while excusing myself. I demand perfection from everyone else while making endless allowances for my own failures. Give me patience with difficult people, remembering that I am also difficult and others must bear with me. Help me extend the same grace I constantly need for myself. Show me what irritating people reveal about my own heart, not to shame me but to grow me. Teach me to bear others' burdens as you've called me to. Give me compassion for their struggles, knowing I have my own. Help me see difficult people not as obstacles but as opportunities. Amen.

14

Learning from the Saints

Consider the lively examples of the holy fathers, in whom true religion shone, and you shall see how little it is, and almost nothing, which we do now.

—The Christian's Pattern, 1741

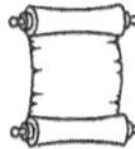

1. Look at the lives of the saints and holy men and women who have gone before us, people in whom real faith actually showed, and then look at our own lives. The gap is humbling. These friends of Christ served Him through hunger and thirst, cold and poverty, exhaustion and sleepless nights, fasting and persecution, and insult after insult (2 Corinthians 11:23–27).
2. Think about what the apostles, martyrs, confessors, and all those who chose to follow Christ actually went through. They considered their lives in this world worthless compared to what was waiting for them (John 12:25). They walked away from wealth, status, honor, friends, and family. They wanted nothing this world had to offer.
3. They used every hour well. Time spent in prayer and contemplation never felt long enough; they were so caught up in God they forgot to eat. They stayed humble, kept loving, kept patient, and moved forward spiritually every single day.
4. They had almost nothing in material terms but were rich in grace (James 2:5). The world didn't know what to do with them, but God called them His own (James 4:4). They thought nothing of themselves, and the world thought

nothing of them, but they were precious to God and deeply loved (1 Peter 2:4).

5. Lord, help me serve you faithfully today, and let today be the day I actually start because everything up to now has been so little (Psalm 90:12). Real spiritual progress doesn't come from our own cleverness; it comes from leaning on the grace of God in everything we do (Proverbs 16:9). And whatever you do, don't just sit there doing nothing but read, write, pray, think, or do something useful for someone else (1 Thessalonians 5:17).
6. The spiritual progress of righteous people depends not so much on their own wisdom as on the grace of God, on whom they must always rely in whatever they undertake (Proverbs 16:9).
7. Never be completely idle. Always be reading or writing or praying or meditating or doing something useful for others (1 Thessalonians 5:17).

This chapter makes me uncomfortable. And I think it's supposed to. À Kempis holds up the mirror of the early church fathers and mothers—the desert monks and nuns, the martyrs, the radical saints—and asks us to compare our lives to theirs. And honestly? We don't measure up. Not even close.

The early saints endured hunger, cold, persecution, and deprivation. We complain if the church coffee isn't good or the sanctuary is too warm. They spent all day working and much of the night in prayer. We struggle to carve out fifteen minutes for devotions.

But here's where I have to be careful. This chapter isn't meant to crush us with guilt. Their external sacrifices flowed from internal transformation. They weren't trying to earn God's love through extreme asceticism; they were so captivated by God that everything else faded in comparison. That's what we're missing in our comfort-saturated Christianity, not the specific practices of the desert fathers but their utter devotion, their single-minded focus.

The grace here is passage 5: spiritual progress "depends not so much upon their own wisdom as upon the grace of God." I can't manufacture transformation through willpower. But I can show up. I can create space. I can remove obstacles. I can cooperate with grace.

Try this: Pick one practice of the saints this week, like extended prayer, fasting, or an hour of silence. Try it.

Lord, forgive me for my lukewarm, comfortable Christianity. I want the benefits of following you without the cost. The example of the holy fathers exposes how little I'm willing to give up for you. Show me what comforts and distractions are stealing my attention from you. Give me their single-minded devotion. Let me find such sweetness in your presence that everything else loses its appeal. Help me begin today as if all my previous efforts count for nothing. Let my progress depend not on my own wisdom or willpower but on your grace, which I desperately need. Amen.

15

The Power of Solitude and Silence

Seek a convenient time to retire into thyself and think often of the benefits of God. Leave curious questions, and read such matters as may rather give compunction to thy heart than occupation to thy head.

—The Christian's Pattern, 1741

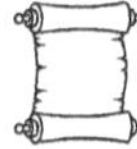

1. Find time to pull back and be quiet (Mark 6:31). Stop chasing controversies and the latest scandals. Read things that actually move your heart, not just fill your head. Cut out the pointless conversations and the unnecessary visits, and stop feeding on news and rumors, and you'll find you have plenty of time to think about what actually matters.
2. Someone once said, "Every time I've been out among people, I came back less of a person than when I left." Most of us know exactly what he meant. Too much time in company costs you something. If you want to grow on the inside, you have to be willing to step away from the crowd and spend real time alone with Jesus (Luke 5:16). Nobody moves safely through the world unless they genuinely love coming home. Nobody speaks safely unless they've learned to be quiet. Nobody leads well unless they've first learned to follow.
3. Even the saints lived with a constant sense of God's holiness and their own smallness. Think about how much peace we'd have if we could just cut out all the noise and fix our minds on God.
4. If you want your heart to be moved, go to your quiet place and shut the world out. The psalmist had it right: "Search

your heart in silence" (Psalm 4:4). What you're always losing out there in the noise, you'll find it in there (Matthew 6:6).

5. In silence and stillness, the soul that loves God grows. Hidden things in Scripture open up. So why do you keep running after things that pull you away? The world is passing away, and everything you crave in it is passing away with it (1 John 2:17).
6. Lift your eyes to God and ask Him to forgive you (Psalm 121:1–2). Leave empty things to people who want empty things. Do what God is asking you to do. Shut your door, call Jesus your beloved into that space (Song of Solomon 5:2), and stay there. You won't find that kind of peace anywhere else (John 14:27).

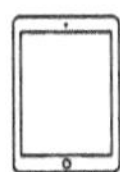

This chapter hits differently in our hyperconnected age. À Kempis is calling us to solitude and silence, two things that terrify most modern people. We've lost the ability to be alone with our thoughts, much less alone with God. The moment we have a free minute, we grab our phones.

But here's what kills me: "As often as I have been among men, I returned less a man," meaning diminished, drained, and less than I was. How often do I experience that? I go out, I engage, I perform, I interact, and I come home spiritually depleted.

The promise in passage 4 stops me in my tracks: "In your prayer closet, you will find what you often lose when you're out and about." What am I losing in the noise and chaos? Clarity. Peace. A sense of God's presence. I go out spiritually full and come home spiritually empty, wondering why I feel so distant from God.

I need to confess something. As someone who's naturally introverted, I LOVE solitude and silence. But this chapter isn't just for introverts. Brian Heasley in his book *Be Still* reminds us that when we approach God in this way, we're "approaching a loving and wild yet stable God; he is full of surprises but going nowhere! He waits for me, he draws me deeper, he calls me to adventure."[5] That's the promise of the prayer closet, not boredom or obligation but encountering the God who is simultaneously safe and dangerous. Solitude isn't the absence of life; it's where we find Life Himself.

Try this: Block fifteen minutes of solitude today. No phone, no agenda. Just show up and see what happens.

Lord, I confess I'm addicted to noise and terrified of silence. I fill every moment with distraction because being alone with you feels uncomfortable. Forgive me. Teach me to love solitude, not as isolation but as intimacy with you. Help me withdraw from the chaos to hear your voice. Give me the courage to silence my phone and actually be still. Show me what I'm trading away in all the noise—the peace, the clarity, and the sense of your presence. Make my prayer closet a place I crave not dread. Stay with me there. Make silence sweet instead of scary. Amen.

5. Heasley, Brian. Be Still: A Simple Guide to Quiet Times. David C Cook, 2022.

16

Conviction of Heart

If thou wilt make any progress, keep thyself in the fear of God, and restrain thyself from too much liberty; for the levity of the mind, and negligence of our faults, maketh us lose the sense of our inward state.

—The Christian's Pattern, 1741

1. If you want to grow spiritually, keep yourself in a reverent awareness of God and don't give yourself too much slack (Proverbs 28:14). Keep your senses in check. Don't drift into foolishness for the sake of a good time.
2. A wandering mind and a casual attitude toward our own faults are what kills our spiritual awareness. We laugh when we should be broken (James 4:9). There's no real freedom or genuine joy apart from a reverent heart and a clear conscience (1 Timothy 1:19).
3. Stay out of other people's business. Look at yourself first; deal with your own stuff before you start correcting anyone else (Matthew 7:5). If people don't think well of you, that's okay. What should actually bother you is whether you're living the way a servant of God should (Galatians 1:10).
4. It's usually better for us not to have too many comforts, especially the worldly kind. But when it comes to spiritual comfort, the reason we rarely experience it is our own fault. We never fully let go of the cheap substitutes.
5. If you thought about your own death as often as you think about living a long life, you'd be a lot more motivated to change (Hebrews 9:27).
6. It doesn't matter where you go or where you turn; you'll be miserable until you turn to God. So why do you keep put-

ting it off? Get up. Start now. Say it out loud: "Now is the time. Right now. Today" (Ephesians 5:16). Because unless you're willing to push hard against your old patterns, sin will keep winning (Matthew 11:12).

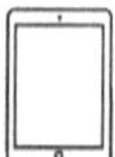

Compunction. Not a word we use much anymore, is it? It means a pricking of conscience, a deep conviction about sin, a holy discomfort with our spiritual condition. À Kempis says we need it if we're going to make any progress.

But here's our problem: "The levity of our minds and want of concern for our faults make us lose the sense of our inward state." We're perpetually entertained, constantly distracted, and always laughing when we should be examining ourselves.

I think about how much energy I spend managing my image. À Kempis flips this, saying "If you don't have people's approval, don't grieve over it, but do grieve that you haven't conducted yourself as carefully and wisely as someone serving God should." Stop worrying about what people think. Start worrying about whether you're actually living like someone who serves God.

And then there's the urgency of passage 6. This is what I learned from a transformational conference experience. Nicky Gumbel walked to center stage and opened with four electrifying words, "NOW is the time!"[6] That's what à Kempis is saying here. Not someday when you feel ready. Not eventually when circumstances improve. NOW. This instant. Get up. Begin.

Try this: What have you been postponing? Do the first step. Today. Right now.

---

6. Gumbel, Nicky. Address at the Alpha Leadership Conference. Royal Albert Hall, London, 2017.

Lord, forgive me for my spiritual escapism. I laugh when I should weep. I'm entertained when I should be examining myself. Give me compunction, that holy discomfort with my sin, that conviction that drives me to change. Don't let me be content with comfortable mediocrity. Expose the empty comforts I cling to that keep me from experiencing divine consolation. Let the reality of death and judgment motivate me to change now not someday. Help me do violence to my old patterns, resist with determination, and begin this very moment. The time is now. Help me arise and begin. Amen.

17

Finishing Well

This life will soon be at an end. Consider, therefore, what it is, and how thou standest, as to thy life hereafter: for to-day a man is, and to-morrow he will be seen no more.

—*The Christian's Pattern, 1741*

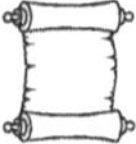

1. This life is almost over. Think carefully about where you stand for the next one (Hebrews 9:27). You're here today and gone tomorrow, and people forget you faster than you'd expect. Live every day like it's your last (Luke 12:40). A clean conscience makes death a lot less scary. Stop sinning; that's better than spending your energy dreading the end.
2. Tomorrow isn't guaranteed; you don't even know if you'll see it. A long life doesn't mean much if you barely grow during it. Living longer doesn't make you better. It often just gives you more time to rack up regrets.
3. Every morning, remind yourself you might not make it to evening. Every evening, don't count on waking up tomorrow (James 4:14). Stay ready. Don't let death catch you off guard.
4. The wisest, most fortunate person is the one who works right now to become who they want to be when they die. While you're healthy you can do a lot. When you're sick, who knows?
5. Don't count on friends and family to sort out your soul. Stop putting it off. If you don't deal with it now, nobody's going to deal with it for you later. This moment matters.

Today is the day of salvation. Right now is the time (2 Corinthians 6:2).

6. What a fool, sitting there thinking you have plenty of time when you can't even promise yourself tomorrow. People get blindsided by death every single day. Someone died in an accident. Someone drowned. Someone collapsed at work. Someone died at the dinner table, laughing one minute, gone the next. Fire. Violence. Sudden illness. Death doesn't check your schedule first. And life? It passes like a shadow (Psalm 144:4).
7. Once you're gone, who's going to remember you? Do what you need to do right now, while you still can because you don't know when your time runs out. While you have the chance, put your energy into what lasts (Luke 12:33). Keep your mind on your soul's salvation. Let everything else take a back seat.

Nobody likes talking about death. We'd rather avoid it, postpone thinking about it, or distract ourselves from its inevitability. But à Kempis forces us to look it in the face; "This life will soon be at an end." Not might be. Will be. And sooner than we think.

The medieval practice of *memento mori*, "remember death" wasn't morbid. It was realistic. It was clarifying. When you remember you're going to die, suddenly the things you're obsessing over don't seem quite so important. The grudge you're nursing, the status you're chasing, the comfort you're clinging to, none of it matters at the deathbed.

The line that haunts me is "When that last hour comes, you will have a far different opinion of your whole life." What seems so important now—the career success, the financial security, the reputation—will all look trivial. What we neglected—relationships, character, spiritual growth, loving God and others—will suddenly be the only things that mattered.

Steve Jobs, in his famous Stanford commencement address, said, "Remembering that I'll be dead soon is the most important tool I've ever encountered to help me make the big choices in life. Because almost everything—all external expectations, all pride, all fear of embarrassment or failure—these things just fall away in the face of death, leaving only what is truly important."[7] À Kempis would agree.

Try this: Write down one thing death would clarify for you. Then live today like it's already clear.

Lord, I don't like thinking about death. I avoid it and distract myself from it. But I'm going to die. And I don't know when. Help me live with that awareness, not in fear but in wisdom. Let remembering death clarify my priorities. Forgive me for living like I have infinite time, for putting off repentance and delaying obedience. Today is all I have. Give me the wisdom to live now as I'll wish I had at the end. Help me invest in eternal things rather than chasing temporary success. Keep my conscience clear so I won't fear death. Make me ready, not someday but today. Amen.

7. Jobs, Steve. Stanford Commencement Address, Stanford, California, June 12, 2005.

18

Facing Judgment

In all things, remember the end and how thou wilt stand before a strict judge, from whom nothing is hidden, who is not bribed with gifts, nor accepteth excuses, but will judge righteousness.

—The Christian's Pattern, 1741

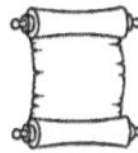

1. In everything you do, keep the end in mind. One day you'll stand before a Judge who sees everything and misses nothing (Hebrews 4:13). You can't bribe Him. You can't talk your way out. He judges on the basis of what's actually true (Romans 2:6). So why aren't you getting ready? On that day, there are no lawyers, no character witnesses, and no one to speak up for you. You stand alone and answer for your own life (Romans 14:12).
2. What fuels the fire of judgment but sin? The more you indulge yourself now and give your desires whatever they want, the harder the reckoning later (Romans 2:5). What you sinned in, you'll be judged in.
3. Grieve your sins now so you can stand with confidence on that day (Matthew 25:34). Because the righteous will stand tall in front of the very people who looked down on them and laughed. The poor and the humble will hold their heads high. The proud will be terrified (Luke 1:52–53).
4. That's the day it becomes obvious who was actually wise, and it's the ones who were willing to look foolish and be written off for Christ's sake (1 Corinthians 3:18). Every hardship endured patiently will turn to joy. The people

who denied themselves will be far happier than those who lived for pleasure.

5. Say you spent your whole life comfortable and prosperous; what does any of it matter if you die tonight? Everything is meaningless except loving God and serving Him (Ecclesiastes 1:2). But those who love God with everything they have? They're not afraid of death, not afraid of judgment, not afraid of anything (1 John 4:18).

Let me be honest, I don't like this chapter. And you probably don't either. We don't talk about judgment and hell much anymore. It feels harsh, medieval, and out of step with our therapeutic culture.

But here's what à Kempis forces us to confront: There are consequences. Actions matter. The way we live now has eternal implications. God is not just a loving Father; He's also a righteous Judge. And "nothing is hidden" from Him.

The warning about storing up punishment is uncomfortable; "The more you spare yourself now and follow the flesh, the greater your punishment will be." What I'm feeding now, whether godliness or selfishness, is what I'll face later.

But notice the flip side. This isn't ultimately about fear; it's about reversal. The righteous will "stand with great boldness." Those who were oppressed will be vindicated. Everything gets turned upside down. The values we chase now, status, comfort, wealth, and power, will be exposed as empty. The things we neglect, humility, suffering for Christ, and simplicity, will be shown as glorious.

Try this: Name one thing you're chasing that won't matter at the end. Begin loosening your grip on it today.

Lord, I confess I don't like thinking about judgment. I'd rather focus on your love without considering your justice. But I will stand before you, and nothing is hidden from you. Forgive me for living as if my choices don't have eternal consequences. Help me prepare now for that day, not in terror but in readiness. Give me the courage to be considered a fool for your sake, knowing that what looks wise now will be shown foolish then. Teach me to love you with my whole heart, so I won't fear death or judgment. When I stand before you, may I hear "Well done." Amen.

19

All In: Wholehearted Devotion

When one that was in great anxiety of mind, often wavering between fear and hope, did once, humbly prostrate himself in prayer, and said, O if I knew that I should persevere! he presently heard within him an answer from God, saying, If thou knewest it, What wouldst thou do?

—*The Christian's Pattern, 1741*

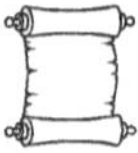

1. Someone was once wrestling with terrible anxiety, caught between fear and hope, and threw himself down in prayer crying out, "If only I knew I would make it to the end!" And immediately he heard something from God deep inside, ""If you knew, what would you do? Do that. Do it now. And you'll be safe" (Matthew 7:24). That was enough. He handed himself over completely to God's will, and the anxiety lifted.
2. "Trust in the Lord and do good," says the psalmist, "and you will live safely in the land" (Psalm 37:3). What holds most people back from real spiritual growth? Fear of the hard work involved. But the people who grow the most are the ones who push hardest through the things that are most difficult for them. We grow the most and receive the most grace right at the point where we overcome ourselves and stop giving in (Galatians 5:24).
3. Learn something wherever you are. When you see or hear of someone living well, push yourself to follow their example (Hebrews 6:12). When you see something worth criticizing, make sure you're not doing the same thing yourself.
4. Remember what you've committed to. Keep the image of your crucified Savior in front of you (Hebrews 12:2).

> When you look honestly at the life of Jesus, you have every reason to be humbled by how little you've tried to become like Him. A believer who seriously meditates on the life and suffering of Christ will find everything they need; nothing better exists beyond Jesus Himself (Colossians 2:3). If the crucified Christ truly took up residence in our hearts, how fast we'd learn everything worth knowing (John 14:26).

This final chapter of Book One brings us full circle. It's about going all in, no half measures, no holding back, wholehearted devotion to God.

The story at the beginning is brilliant. Someone's anxious, wavering, wondering, "What if I don't persevere?" And God's answer is perfect: "If you knew you would persevere, what would you do? Do that now." Stop worrying about the future. Stop trying to figure everything out. Just do now what you know you should do. Live today as if you already have the assurance you're seeking. The person "committed himself wholly to the will of God, and his anxiety ceased."

I love the honesty in passage 2: "One thing there is that draws many back from spiritual progress and diligent amendment: the horror of the difficulty or the labor of the combat." Translation: spiritual growth is hard, and we don't like hard things. But growth doesn't happen in comfort; it happens in resistance.

À Kempis ends with a gut-punch: "You have good cause to be ashamed when you look at the life of Jesus Christ, seeing that you haven't tried harder to conform yourself to Him, though you've walked in the way of God for a long time." How long have I been a Christian? And how little do I actually look like Jesus? But notice, He doesn't leave us in shame; He gives us hope. Everything we need is found in Jesus. Just Jesus. Crucified, risen, present.

Try this: Name one thing you're trusting more than Jesus. Hand it over today. He's been waiting.

Lord Jesus, I confess I'm often not all in. I hold back. I hedge my bets. I want the benefits of following you without the cost. Forgive me. Help me to stop worrying about the future and start obeying in the present. Show me where I'm avoiding difficulty, taking the easy path, and neglecting the hard work of spiritual combat. Give me courage to face what's contrary to me; that's where I'll grow most. I'm ashamed of how long I've walked with you and how little I look like you. But everything I need is found in you. Make me wholehearted in my devotion. Whatever it takes, whatever it costs, I'm yours. Amen.

THE CHRISTIAN'S PATTERN – BOOK TWO

THE INNER LIFE

20

The Inner Life

The kingdom of God is within you, saith the Lord. Turn thee with thy whole heart unto the Lord, and forsake this wretched world, and thy soul shall find rest.

—***The Christian's Pattern*, 1741**

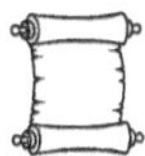

1. "The kingdom of God is within you," says the Lord (Luke 17:21). Turn to the Lord with all your heart, leave this miserable world behind, and your soul will find rest (Matthew 11:29). Learn to turn away from outward things and give yourself to inward things, and you'll see the kingdom of God come within you.
2. The kingdom of God is peace and joy in the Holy Spirit (Romans 14:17). Christ will come to you and show you His consolation if you prepare a worthy dwelling place for Him within (John 14:23).
3. He often visits the inward person, has sweet conversations with them, and gives pleasant comfort, much peace, and amazing intimacy.
4. Come, faithful soul, prepare your heart for this Bridegroom (Revelation 3:20). He says, "If anyone loves me, my Father will love them, and we will make our home with them" (John 14:23). Give Christ room and deny entrance to everything else. When you have Christ, you're rich. He is enough.
5. People change quickly and fail you fast. But Christ remains forever and stands by you faithfully to the end (Hebrews 13:8). Don't place great trust in a frail mortal. Those who

are with you today may be against you tomorrow (Proverbs 27:10). Put all your trust in God; let Him be the object of your fear and your love (Psalm 31:14).

6. You have no lasting city here (Hebrews 13:14), and wherever you are, you're a stranger and pilgrim (1 Peter 2:11). You'll never have rest unless you're deeply united with Christ. Your true home is in heaven. Be careful not to cling to earthly things, or you'll perish with them (Colossians 3:2).
7. Let your thoughts be on the Most High and direct your prayers to Christ without ceasing (1 Thessalonians 5:17). If you can't contemplate heavenly things, rest in the passion of Christ and dwell in His holy wounds. You'll feel great comfort in tribulation and easily bear the criticism of others (1 Peter 2:24).
8. Christ was despised and, in His greatest need, was forsaken by His friends (Mark 14:50). Christ chose to suffer—how dare you complain about anything? If you're unwilling to suffer anything, how will you be a friend of Christ (James 1:12)? Suffer with Christ if you want to reign with Him (2 Timothy 2:12).
9. If you'd ever tasted a little of Jesus' burning love, you wouldn't care about your own advantage or disadvantage. You'd rejoice even when people insult you because the love of Jesus makes a person forget themselves (Philippians 2:3).
10. The person who sees things as they truly are, not as people say they are, is truly wise and taught by God (1 John 2:27). An interior person quickly gathers themselves for prayer because they're never completely absorbed by outward things.
11. No outward work or necessary business hinders them. Those who are well-ordered within don't care about people's strange behavior. We're hindered only to the degree that we're pulled into external things.
12. If all were well with you and you were thoroughly purified, everything would work together for your good (Romans 8:28). Nothing defiles and entangles the human heart like impure love for created things (1 John 2:15).

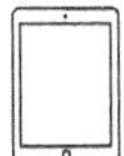

Welcome to Book Two. If Book One was about the outer life, our actions and disciplines, Book Two is about the inner life. And honestly? This is where it gets real.

"The kingdom of God is within you" (Luke 17:21). Not out there. Not in external religious practices. Within.

The promise is beautiful; "Christ will come to you if you prepare a worthy place for him within." But preparing that place means evicting other tenants, such as ambition, approval-seeking, comfort-chasing, worry, and control. Christ says, give me room, deny entrance to everything else.

The final warning is sobering; "nothing defiles and entangles the human heart like disordered attachment to created things." We think our problem is out there. But the real problem is within us.

Where is your mind dwelling? On outward things or inward things? On Christ or on everything else?

Try this: Today, when your mind drifts outward, bring it back. Do that once, just once, on purpose.

Lord Jesus, the kingdom of God is within me, but I keep looking for it everywhere else. I chase outward things while neglecting the interior life. Forgive me. Come and make your home in me, but help me prepare a worthy dwelling first. Evict my little idols, my comfort seeking, my need for approval, my desperation for control. Teach me not to place my ultimate trust in people, who change and disappoint, but in you alone, who stand by me faithfully to the end. Help me see things as they truly are, not as they are valued by others. Purify my heart from disordered attachment to created things, and make me an interior person deeply united with you. Amen.

21
Humble Surrender

Beware therefore thou lean not too much upon any desire conceived without asking my counsel, lest perhaps afterwards it repent thee, and thou dislike what before pleased thee.

—*The Christian's Pattern, 1741*

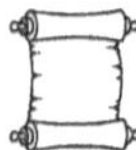

1. Don't worry too much about who's for you or against you. Instead, work to ensure that God is with you in everything you do (Romans 8:31). Keep a good conscience, and God will defend you (1 Peter 3:16). No one can harm those whom God helps. If you can hold your peace and suffer without complaining, you'll undoubtedly see the Lord's deliverance (Exodus 14:14). He knows the time and manner to deliver you so resign yourself to Him (Psalm 37:5). It's God's job to help and deliver you from all shame. It's often good for keeping us humble that others know and criticize our faults.
2. When someone humbles themselves because of their faults, they easily satisfy those who are offended (Matthew 5:23–24). He reveals His secrets to the humble and sweetly draws them to Himself (Matthew 11:25). The humble person, though they suffer shame, is still at peace because they rest in God, not in the world's approval (Colossians 3:3). Don't think you've made any spiritual progress unless you consider yourself inferior to everyone else.

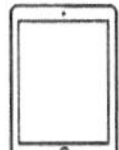

Humble surrender. Two words that feel completely backward in our self-promoting, personal-branding, hustle-culture world. We're told to advocate for ourselves, to fight for what we deserve, and to make sure everyone knows our worth. And here's à Kempis saying: "Don't worry too much about who's for you or against you. Instead, work to ensure that God is with you in everything you do." That's a radical reorientation. Stop tracking who's on your side. Stop keeping score of who's supporting you and who's not. Just make sure God's with you. That's it.

When someone criticizes me, my immediate response is to defend myself, to explain why they're wrong, and to protect my reputation. But à Kempis says God will defend me. That's His job, not mine.

I learned this the hard way early in my current appointment. Through ignorance and poor advice, I made a decision that set off a firestorm. I was terrified. Overwhelmed. Every instinct screamed at me to defend myself, to explain, to fix it. But in the midst of my panic, I heard the Lord speak Exodus 14:13–14 to my heart: "Stand still, and see the salvation of the Lord... The Lord will fight for you; you need only to be still." So, I didn't say anything. I held my peace. And things just... resolved. The relationship was restored, better than before.

Every good thing in me comes from God. Every accomplishment is by His grace. I have nothing to boast about except the cross (Galatians 6:14). Stop obsessing over your status, your reputation, or your place in the pecking order. Just rest in God.

Try this: Name one thing you're doing today for the approval of others. Do it for God instead. Don't tell anyone.

Lord, I confess I care way too much about who's for me and who's against me. I keep score. I track approval. I manage my reputation and defend myself constantly instead of letting you defend me. Teach me to resign myself to you, not in fatalism but in trust, knowing you know the time and manner to deliver me. Forgive me for managing my image; when my failures are exposed, help me receive it as grace. Draw me to yourself, reveal your secrets to me, and raise me up in your timing. Help me stop obsessing over my status. Make me truly humble, resting in you alone. Amen.

22

Being at Peace

Keep thyself in peace, and then mayest thou pacify others. A peaceable man doth more good than a learned one. A passionate man turneth even good into evil, and easily believeth the worst.

—***The Christian's Pattern, 1741***

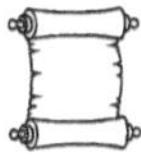

1. First, keep yourself in peace, and then you can bring peace to others (Matthew 5:9). A peaceable person does more good than someone who's well educated. A hot-headed person turns even good into evil and easily believes the worst, but a peaceable person turns all things into good. Those who are at peace aren't suspicious of anyone (1 Corinthians 13:7). But those who are discontented aren't quiet themselves and won't let others be quiet either. They often say things they shouldn't say and fail to do things they should do. They focus on what others are supposed to do but neglect their own responsibilities.
2. Therefore, have careful concern for yourself first, and then you can rightly be concerned for your neighbor (Matthew 7:5).
3. You're really good at excusing your own actions but won't accept others' excuses. It would be more just to accuse yourself and excuse your brother (Romans 2:1). If you want people to put up with you, you need to put up with them too. Look how far you still are from Christ-like love and humility, which doesn't know how to be angry with anyone except oneself. It's no great accomplishment to get along with good and gentle people; everyone enjoys peace with like-minded people (Luke 6:32–33). But to be able to

live peaceably with difficult, disorderly people or those who oppose us, that's a great grace (Matthew 5:44).

4. Some people keep themselves in peace and maintain peace with others. And there are some who are neither at peace themselves nor let others be at peace. They're forever stirring up trouble with others but are always more troublesome to themselves. Others keep themselves in peace and work to bring others to peace.
5. Yet our whole peace in this miserable life consists more in humbly enduring suffering than in not feeling adversity (James 1:2–4). Those who know best how to suffer will keep themselves in greater peace. They're conquerors of themselves, masters of the world, friends of Christ, and heirs of heaven (Romans 8:17).

"First, keep yourself in peace, and then you can bring peace to others." This hits me hard because I'm constantly trying to fix everyone else while ignoring my own chaos. And you can't give what you don't have.

À Kempis says a peaceable person does more good than someone who's well educated. That's convicting. I can have all the theological training, all the biblical knowledge, all the right answers, but if I'm anxious and reactive and stirring up trouble, what good is any of it?

I'm laser-focused on what everyone else should be doing while neglecting my own responsibilities. I see their faults clearly but excuse my own when "it would be more just to accuse yourself and excuse your brother." Be harsh with yourself and generous with others. But we do the opposite, generous with ourselves and harsh with everyone else.

À Kempis identifies three kinds of people: those who keep themselves in peace and are at peace with others; those who aren't at peace themselves and won't let anyone else be either, forever stirring up trouble but always more troublesome to themselves; and those who keep themselves in peace and actively work to bring others to peace. If I'm honest, I fluctuate. Sometimes I'm the peacemaker. Too often I'm the second type, discontented and spreading it around.

"Those who know best how to suffer will keep themselves in greater peace." The person who's learned to endure hardship without complaining, without losing their center, and without taking it out on everyone else, that person has found real peace. And that person? "They're conquerors of themselves, masters of the world, friends of Christ, and heirs of heaven."

Try this: Find one thing that's annoying you right now. Practice enduring it quietly. Don't mention it to anyone.

Lord, I want to bring peace to others, but I'm not at peace myself. I'm anxious, reactive, and easily stirred up. Forgive me for trying to fix everyone else while my own soul is in chaos. Teach me to keep myself in peace first, before I try to fix everyone else. Show me how harsh I am with others and how lenient with myself, and help me flip them. Give me grace to live peaceably, not just with agreeable people but with difficult, disorderly, opposing people. Teach me that peace isn't the absence of adversity but the ability to suffer well, staying centered in you when everything around me is chaos. Make me a peacemaker, a conqueror of myself, and a friend of Christ. Amen.

23

Pure Motives

Simplicity and purity are the two wings by which a man is lifted above all earthly things. Simplicity must be in his intention, purity in his affections.

—The Christian's Pattern, 1741

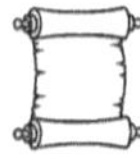

1. Simplicity and purity are the two wings by which we rise above all earthly things (Hebrews 12:1). Simplicity is about what you aim for; purity is about what you love. Simplicity reaches toward God; purity takes hold of Him and experiences Him (Matthew 5:8). No good action will hinder you if you're inwardly free from disordered attachments. If you intend and seek nothing but God's will and your neighbor's good, you'll enjoy true inner freedom (Galatians 5:13).
2. When your heart is right, every created thing becomes a window to God—a mirror of life and a lesson in His character (Romans 1:20). There's no creature so small and insignificant that it doesn't point to His goodness. A pure heart sees clearly and understands without effort (Titus 1:15). You see the world through the lens of your own heart. Where there's joy in the world, the pure-hearted person finds it. Where there's trouble and suffering, a guilty conscience feels it most (Proverbs 28:1).
3. Iron thrown into fire loses its rust and comes out bright and strong, and that's what happens when we turn ourselves completely toward God. The spiritual rust burns away. The apathy, the disordered loves, are gone. We're changed into His likeness (2 Corinthians 3:18). But the moment we start going lukewarm, the first thing to go is our willingness to push through.

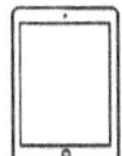

Simplicity and purity. Two words that feel almost quaint in our complex, sophisticated world. We value nuance, strategy, and positioning. We're multi-layered, multi-faceted, and managing multiple personas across multiple platforms. Simplicity feels naive. Purity feels impossible.

But à Kempis says these are the "two wings by which we rise above all earthly things." Simplicity in intention—what you're aiming for. Purity in affection—what you love. "If you intend and seek nothing but the will of God and the good of your neighbor, you will enjoy true inner freedom." That's the promise. Real freedom comes from having one goal (God's will) and one concern (your neighbor's good). Not ten goals. Not a hundred competing priorities. Just those two.

But we complicate everything. We want God's will plus our comfort. Our neighbor's good plus our reputation. We layer in self-interest, self-protection, and self-advancement, and then wonder why we feel tangled up and stuck.

The image of iron in fire is perfect. Iron covered in rust looks dead and useless. But put it in the fire and the rust burns away, becoming bright, useful, and transformed. That's what happens when we "wholly turn ourselves to God." The spiritual rust, apathy, lukewarmness, and disordered loves, burns away. We're purified and "changed into the likeness of God."

Try this: Before your next act of service, check your motive. If it's mixed, do it anyway, and ask God to purify it.

Lord, I'm so complicated. My intentions are mixed. My motives are murky. I want your will, but I also want my comfort. I want my neighbor's good, but I also want my reputation protected. I'm tangled up in a hundred competing desires, and I've lost my freedom. Give me simplicity of intention. Help me want one thing, your will, not your will plus my comfort. Purify my affections; burn away the rust of spiritual apathy and disordered loves. Give me a pure heart so I can see you everywhere, in birds and trees, in setbacks and joys, in all of creation. Help me overcome myself so that what once seemed impossible becomes natural. Transform me not through my effort but through your fire. Amen.

24
Know Yourself

We cannot trust much to ourselves because we have often neither grace nor understanding. There is but little light in us, and that we quickly lose by negligence.

—*The Christian's Pattern, 1741*

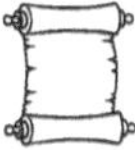

1. We shouldn't trust ourselves too much because we often lack both grace and understanding (Proverbs 3:5). There's only a little light in us, and what we have, we quickly lose through carelessness (Matthew 25:8). We criticize small things in others but overlook greater faults in ourselves (Matthew 7:3). Those who rightly consider their own actions will find little reason to judge others harshly.
2. The inward Christian puts caring for themselves before all other concerns (Matthew 16:26). Those who diligently attend to themselves easily maintain peace concerning others. You'll never be truly spiritual unless you stop obsessing over other people's business and pay special attention to yourself (Galatians 6:4). If you give your full attention to God and yourself, you'll be minimally affected by whatever you see happening around you.
3. Where are you when you're not present with yourself? And when you've examined everyone and everything else, what have you gained if you've neglected yourself (Mark 8:36)? If you want peace of mind, you must set aside all other concerns and attend to your own spiritual condition (Philippians 4:7). You'll make much progress if you keep yourself free from all temporal cares. You'll fail badly if you

value anything in this world too highly. Let nothing seem great, high, or pleasing to you except God Himself or what comes from God (Colossians 3:2). Consider all comfort from any created thing to be empty and vain.

4. A soul that loves God despises everything except God. God alone, who is everlasting, immense, and filling all things, is the comfort of the soul and the true joy of the heart (Psalm 73:25–26).

"We shouldn't trust ourselves too much because we often lack both grace and understanding." That's a hard pill to swallow in a culture that tells us to "trust yourself," "follow your heart," and "you do you." We're told our feelings are always valid, our instincts are always right, and our perspective is our truth. But à Kempis says, "You lack both grace and understanding." You're not as wise as you think. Your judgment is flawed. Your perspective is limited. You need God's grace and God's wisdom because yours isn't enough.

And here's the kicker: "We quickly notice and dwell on what we suffer from others, but we don't pay attention to what others suffer from us." I remember every slight, every offense, and every time you hurt me. But what about all the times I hurt you? Somehow those don't register as vividly.

The call to self-focus sounds selfish at first; "The inward Christian puts caring for themselves before all other concerns." But it's not selfishness—it's priority. You can't help others well if you haven't dealt with yourself. You can't bring peace to others if you're not at peace. You can't offer grace if you haven't received it.

Everything else, comfort from created things, approval from people, and success by the world's standards, is empty. Not necessarily evil but empty. It won't satisfy. It won't last. Only God is "everlasting, immense, filling all things;" only He is the "comfort of the soul, and the true joy of the heart."

Try this: Spend five minutes today not seeking anything from God. Just be with Him. No agenda.

Lord, I confess I trust myself too much. I think my judgment is sound, my perspective is right, and my feelings are valid. Forgive my arrogance. Help me see my own faults as clearly as I see others' and be as generous with their failures as I am with my own. Teach me to focus on myself first, not in selfishness but in responsibility, dealing with my own soul before trying to fix everyone else's. Free me from passing worries. Help me set aside all other concerns to attend to you and my own spiritual condition. You alone are the comfort of my soul and the true joy of my heart. Amen.

25

A Clear Conscience

The glory of a good man is the testimony of a good conscience. Have a good conscience, and thou shalt always have joy. A good conscience is able to bear very much and is very cheerful in adversity.

—The Christian's Pattern, 1741

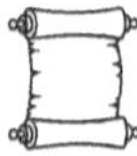

1. The mark of a good person is a good conscience (2 Corinthians 1:12). Get that right and joy follows. When your heart doesn't condemn you, you sleep well (1 John 3:21). Don't celebrate unless you've actually done well. People living in unrepented sin never have real joy or genuine peace because "there is no peace for the wicked," says the Lord (Isaiah 48:22).
2. When you love God, even suffering can become a source of joy because to embrace suffering for His sake is to share in the cross of Christ (Galatians 6:14)
3. Human praise doesn't last (John 5:44). Sorrow always follows worldly success. Real glory lives in your conscience, not in what people say about you. The joy of the righteous comes from God and is grounded in truth (Psalm 97:11). The person who doesn't need anyone's approval, who can take praise or criticism and stay steady, enjoys deep peace (Galatians 1:10. A clear conscience makes contentment easy. You're not holier because someone praised you, and you're not worse because someone criticized you (Proverbs 27:21). You are what you are before God, nothing more, nothing less (1 Samuel 16:7). When you're honest about who you really are on the inside, what other people say

stops mattering. People look at the outside; God looks at the heart. People judge what you did; God weighs why you did it (1 Chronicles 28:9).

4. Doing good consistently while thinking little of yourself, that's what a humble soul looks like. The person who doesn't need outside validation has learned to rest entirely in God (2 Corinthians 10:18). As Paul put it, it's not the person who promotes themselves who gets God's approval; it's the person God commends (2 Corinthians 10:18). To walk closely with God and hold nothing above Him, that's what it means to be truly spiritual.

A clear conscience. That's what this chapter is about. And honestly? Most of us don't have one. We're carrying guilt, shame, and regret. We're haunted by what we've done and what we've left undone. We're anxious about what people think. We're performing for approval. We're managing our image. And we wonder why we don't have joy.

À Kempis says, "Have a good conscience, and you'll always have joy." Not have a perfect life or have everyone's approval or have all your problems solved. Just a good conscience. That's the key to joy.

But here's what kills me, "Never celebrate unless you've done well." We celebrate all kinds of things, promotions, purchases, accomplishments, while our conscience is screaming at us. We party while we're morally bankrupt, and we wonder why the joy feels hollow.

"Sinners never have true joy or feel inward peace." That's not self-righteousness; it's reality. When you're living in unrepented sin, you can have pleasure, distraction, entertainment, but not joy. Not peace. There's always that nagging sense that something's wrong.

Try this: Name one thing your conscience has been nudging you about. Deal with it before you go to bed tonight.

Lord, I confess my conscience isn't clear. I'm carrying guilt, shame, and regret. I've done things I shouldn't have and left undone things I should have. Cleanse my conscience with your blood and give me true joy, the kind that comes from a clear conscience, not from entertainment or distraction. Free me from caring what people think; I am what I am before you, and your opinion is the only one that matters. You see my heart, not just my face; you weigh my intentions, not just my deeds, so purify my motives. Teach me to walk inwardly with you, holding nothing above you. Approve me, Lord. Let your approval be enough. Amen.

26

Loving Jesus Above All

Blessed is he that knoweth what it is to love Jesus, and to despise himself for Jesus' sake. Thou must give up a beloved friend for the love of thy beloved, for Jesus will be loved alone above all things.

—The Christian's Pattern, 1741

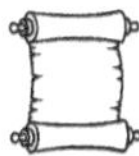

1. Blessed are those who understand what it is to love Jesus and deny themselves for His sake (Luke 14:26). You must give up what you love for Jesus, for He must be loved above all (Matthew 10:37). The love of created things is deceptive and unreliable; the love of Jesus is faithful and constant (Hebrews 13:8). Those who cling to created things will fall with them; those who embrace Jesus will stand firm forever (Psalm 146:3–4). Love Him and make Him your friend; He won't abandon you when everyone else leaves (John 6:67–68). One day, everyone will leave you, whether you want them to or not.
2. Stay close to Jesus, both in life and death, and trust His faithfulness; when all others fail, He alone can help you (2 Timothy 4:16–17). Jesus won't share you with anyone else; He wants your whole heart and will rule there as king (Exodus 20:3). Any love you give to anyone or anything other than Jesus is wasted (1 John 2:15). Don't trust or depend on a broken reed, for all people are like grass, and all their glory will fade (Isaiah 40:6–7).
3. You'll quickly be deceived if you only look at people's outward appearance (1 Samuel 16:7). If you look to others for comfort and advantage, you'll often be disappointed (Jeremiah 17:5). For if you don't seek Jesus, you hurt yourself more than the world and all your enemies could (Mark 8:36).

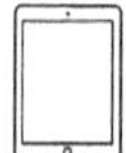

"He must be loved above all." That's the line that stops me in my tracks. Jesus doesn't want to share top billing. He doesn't want to be one option among many. He doesn't want part of your heart while the rest is divided among a dozen other loves. He wants all of it.

À Kempis says that Jesus "won't share you with anyone else; He wants your whole heart and will rule there as king." This is exclusive love. Total devotion. Undivided affection. We don't like that. We want Jesus plus our comfort. Jesus plus our success. Jesus plus our approval from others. Jesus plus whatever else we're clinging to. But He's saying, me alone, or you'll lose everything.

But Jesus? He's faithful. He's constant. He won't leave. When everyone else walks away, and they will, He remains.

"If you seek Jesus in all things, you'll surely find Jesus." There's the promise. He's not hiding. He's not playing games. If you seek Him, you'll find Him. But you have to seek HIM, not yourself with Him as a means to an end. "If you seek yourself, you'll also find yourself but to your own destruction." When Jesus becomes a tool for your self-interest, when Christianity becomes about self-improvement rather than self-denial, when it's all about what you get out of it, you find yourself. But that's not good news. Finding yourself apart from Jesus is destruction.

Try this: Ask yourself honestly: am I following Jesus or following what Jesus can do for me? Sit with the answer.

Lord Jesus, I confess I try to love you alongside a hundred other things. I want you plus my comfort, my success, my approval, and my plans. But you're calling me to love you alone. Forgive me for dividing my heart. Show me where I cling to created things and trust broken reeds. I know you won't tolerate any rivals. Break my disordered attachments and sit as King on the throne of my heart Thank you that your love is faithful and constant when everything else fades. Help me seek you in all things, not myself with you as a means to an end but truly you. You are enough. Amen.

27

Close to Jesus

When Jesus is present, all is well, and nothing seemeth difficult, but when Jesus is absent, everything is hard. When Jesus speaketh not inwardly, we have no comfort worth the name.

—The Christian's Pattern, 1741

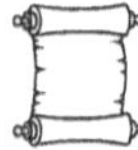

1. When Jesus is present, everything is wonderful. When Jesus is absent, everything is hard (Song of Solomon 5:6). When He doesn't speak to us inwardly, nothing else truly comforts us. But one word form Jesus and everything shifts (John 6:68). Remember how Mary jumped up the moment Martha told her, "The Teacher is here and asking for you" (John 11:28–29)? That's what it's like. Blessed is the moment Jessus calls you out of grief and into joy. Losing Jesus would be a greater loss than losing everything else in the world (Mark 8:36).
2. What does the world have to offer without Jesus? Nothing that lasts. Without Jesus, life is hollow at its core. With Jesus, even the hardest days have something solid underneath them (Philippians 1:23). If Jesus is with you, nothing can ultimately hurt you (Romans 8:31).
3. Finding Jesus is finding the greatest treasure there is (Matthew 13:44). Losing Jesus is losing more than everything. The poorest person on earth is the one without Jesus. The richest is the one close to Him. Stay humble and peaceable and Jesus will be with you. Stay prayerful and still and Jesus will stay. Turn toward outward things and you'll push Him away fast (1 John 2:15). And if you push Him away, where will you go? You can't live well without a true friend,

and if Jesus isn't your closest friend, nothing will fill that space (Proverbs 18:24).

4. Better to have the whole world against you than to offend Jesus (Matthew 10:28). Of everything you hold dear, let Jesus be what you hold dearest. Love everyone, but love them for Jesus' sake and love Jesus for who He is, not for what He gives you (Matthew 22:37). He alone is faithful above every friend (Hebrews 13:8). Love your friends and your enemies both for His sake. Don't chase special recognition or affection from anyone. That belongs to God alone. Don't set your heart on any person. Let Jesus be everything, in you and in everyone around you (Colossians 3:11).
5. Stay free on the inside. Don't let your heart get tangled up with anything created (2 Corinthians 6:17). Without God's grace enabling you, you'll never manage to let go of everything and be fully united to Him (John 15:5). When grace comes, you can do anything. When it withdraws, you feel how small you really are. But don't despair; keep going for Christ's glory. After winter comes summer. After the storm, calm returns (Psalm 30:5).

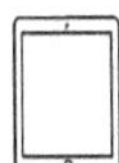

"When Jesus is present, all is well. But when Jesus is absent, everything is hard." There are seasons when Jesus feels close, when prayer is sweet and Scripture leaps off the page. And then there are seasons when He feels absent, when prayer feels like talking to the ceiling and you feel spiritually dry and empty.

À Kempis doesn't say the dry seasons mean you're doing something wrong. He just acknowledges the reality, "When Jesus doesn't speak inwardly, we have no true comfort." Sometimes Jesus is silent, not because He's abandoned you but because He's teaching you to trust Him even when you don't feel Him.

"You're acting foolishly if you trust or rejoice in anyone else." Stop trying to make people, things, or experiences do what only Jesus can do. They'll always disappoint. They can't bear that weight.

"Love all for Jesus, but Jesus for Himself." Love people, yes. But love Jesus, not for what He gives you but for who He is. The dry seasons don't last. Winter gives way to summer. Storms give way to calm. Jesus hasn't abandoned you. He's just teaching you to trust Him in the dark.

Try this: Tell Jesus one thing you're afraid of in the dark right now. Then stay in the conversation a little longer.

Lord Jesus, I confess that when you feel present, everything is easy. But when you feel absent, everything is hard. Forgive me for trying to find in other things what only you can give. Thank you that even when you feel absent, you haven't abandoned me; you're teaching me to trust you in the dark. Help me understand that losing you would be worse than losing everything else. Teach me to love all people for your sake but to love you for yourself alone. When your grace comes, keep me humble; when it withdraws, keep me from despair. After winter comes summer and after a storm, a great calm. Keep me close to you always. Amen.

28

When All Comfort Is Gone

It is not hard to despise human comfort when we have divine. It is much and very much to be able to want both human and divine comfort and, for the glory of GOD, to be willing to endure desolation of spirit.

—*The Christian's Pattern, 1741*

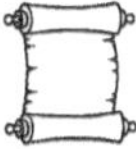

1. It's not that hard to give up human comfort when you have God's comfort (Psalm 73:25–26). What's genuinely hard and genuinely great is when both are gone. When you have no human comfort and no felt sense of God's presence either, and you endure that desolation for His glory anyway (Job 13:15). Anyone can be cheerful and devoted when grace is flowing. That's easy. God's grace carries you, and you barely feel the weight.
2. The truth is we're always looking for something to lean on, and letting go of ourselves is one of the hardest things there is (Luke 9:23). The martyr St. Lawrence overcame the world because nothing in it held any value for him. He loved the Creator more than he loved people and chose what pleased God over what comforted himself. That's the invitation for you too, to give up even someone dear to you for the love of God (Matthew 10:37). Don't fall apart when a friend leaves. We're all going to be separated eventually (Ecclesiastes 3:1–8).
3. People who lean on themselves tend to run straight toward human comfort the moment things get hard. But someone who truly loves Christ learns to endure hard seasons for His sake (2 Timothy 2:3). When God's comfort does come, receive it gratefully, but know it's His gift, not something

you earned (James 1:17). Don't let it make you proud. Let it make you more humble and more careful because it won't last forever and testing always follows (1 Peter 5:6).

4. David said it perfectly: In the good times, "I thought I would never be shaken" (Psalm 30:6). In the hard times, "You hid your face and I was terrified" (Psalm 30:7). But he didn't give up. He prayed harder. And finally, "You turned my mourning into dancing" (Psalm 30:11). That's the arc. Hold on.
5. So where do I turn when grace is gone? Only to the mercy of God (Lamentations 3:21–24). Not to good friends, not to books, not to worship music, all of those help in normal times, but when you're in real desolation, none of it touches the emptiness (Psalm 63:1–3). The only move left is patience and surrender, giving your will to God and waiting (Luke 22:42).
6. Here's something worth knowing: The temptation that hits hardest is often a sign that comfort is on its way (James 1:12). God gives comfort to strengthen you for what's ahead. Then, He allows testing so you don't get proud (2 Corinthians 12:7–9). The enemy never stops. The flesh never fully cooperates. Stay ready (1 Peter 5:8).

This chapter is about spiritual dryness, what the old saints called "desolation." It's when you not only do not feel God's presence, but you also don't have the comfort of friends, books, or anything else. You're spiritually empty, and everything feels pointless.

À Kempis says it's easy to do without human comfort when you have divine comfort. But what about when God feels absent too? "It's much harder, and truly great, to lack both human and divine comfort and for God's glory, to willingly endure desolation of heart." That's the real test.

Passage 5 is painfully honest and hits a little too close to home for someone like me who finds enormous comfort in books; "Good people, religious friends, faithful companions, holy books, excellent writings, or sweet songs and hymns, all these offer little help and bring little comfort when grace forsakes me and I'm left in my own poverty." Even all the good spiritual stuff doesn't help when you're in desolation. Nothing works. You're just... empty.

"At such times, there's no better remedy than patience and surrendering my will to the will of God." That's it. That's the only move. Wait. Surrender. Trust that this season won't last forever.

Try this: Identify the comfort you're most desperately seeking right now. Surrender it. Not forever, just today.

Lord, I confess I'm a comfort addict. I always need something—your presence, people's approval, entertainment, food, and yes, an embarrassing number of books—to make me feel okay. Teach me to be content even when I have nothing. Forgive me for loving you for what you give me rather than who you are. When I'm in desolation, when spiritual dryness hits, and when all comfort is gone, give me patience and help me surrender my will to yours. Don't let me grow proud when comfort comes or despair when it goes. Thank you that after winter comes summer and after a storm, a great calm. You are my only hope. In you alone, I find my rest. Amen.

29

Be Grateful for Grace

Why dost thou seek rest, since thou art born to labor? Dispose thyself to patience rather than to comfort and to the bearing of the cross rather than to joy. Be thankful for the least gift, so thou shalt be worthy to receive greater.

—The Christian's Pattern, 1741

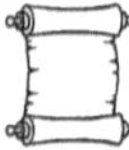

1. Why are you looking for rest when you were born to work? Train yourself to be patient rather than comfortable and to carry the cross rather than chase joy. What person wouldn't want spiritual joy and comfort if they could always have it? Spiritual comfort is greater than anything the world offers. But chasing comfort isn't the path to it.
2. False independence and self-reliance push away God's grace. God does right by giving comfort when He gives it. But we do wrong when we don't return thanks to the Giver. That's why grace can't keep flowing in us; we're not grateful, and we don't give it back to the one it came from. Grace always stays close to the grateful person. What was given to the humble will be taken from the proud. Accept only the grace that makes you more humble, more careful, and more willing to let go of yourself. Anyone truly taught by grace, both when it comes and when it's withdrawn, won't dare take credit for anything good. They'll admit they're poor and empty without God. Give God what belongs to God. Give yourself what belongs to you, which is nothing except sin and its consequences.
3. Always put yourself in the lowest place, and the highest will be given to you. The greatest saints in God's eyes are the least in their own. The more glorious they are, the more

humble they are. Those who are firmly rooted in God can't be proud.

4. Be thankful for the smallest gift, and you'll receive greater ones. Let the least gift seem very great to you, and even the most ordinary seem like something special. When you consider the greatness of the Giver, no gift seems small. What comes from the Most High God is never trivial. Even if He gives you hardship and discipline, be grateful; He allows whatever comes to us for our good. If you want to keep God's grace, be thankful when it comes and patient when it's withdrawn, pray for its return, and stay humble so you don't lose it.

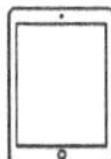

"Be thankful for the smallest gift, and you'll receive greater ones."

We live in a culture of complaint. We notice what's missing more than what's present. We focus on what God hasn't done rather than what He has. And according to this chapter, that's exactly why grace stops flowing.

The chapter makes a striking claim: grace can't keep flowing in us when we're not grateful. Not because God is withholding it but because ingratitude closes us off. A heart full of complaint has no room for grace.

À Kempis is honest about our default mode. We want comfort without the cross, joy without patience, and blessing without discipline. We want God's gifts without God Himself.

The corrective is simple but costly: gratitude. Not just for the big things, the healings, the breakthroughs, the answered prayers, but for the smallest gifts. The cup of coffee. The conversation. The breath in your lungs. When you consider the worth of the Giver, nothing He gives is small.

"Give God what belongs to God. Give yourself what belongs to you, which is nothing except sin and its consequences." That's the posture grace requires. Not self-promotion. Not taking credit. Just honest acknowledgment that everything good came from Him.

The most spiritually mature people aren't the ones with the most impressive testimonies. They're the ones who are genuinely grateful for everything, including the hard things.

Try this: Name three things you've been taking for granted. Thank God for each one out loud, specifically.

God, I confess I'm better at noticing what's missing than what's present. I've been ungrateful for small gifts, impatient when comfort is withdrawn, and quick to take credit when things go well. Forgive me. Teach me to receive everything, including hardship, as coming from your hand for my good. Make me the kind of person who holds grace loosely and returns thanks freely. I have nothing good that didn't come from you. Everything is gift. Help me live like I believe that. Amen.

30

Few Truly Love the Cross

Jesus hath many lovers of His heavenly kingdom but few bearers of His cross. He hath many desirers of comfort but few of tribulation. Many love Jesus so long as no adversity happens. But they who love Jesus for Jesus, and not for some comfort of their own, bless Him in all tribulation.

—***The Christian's Pattern, 1741***

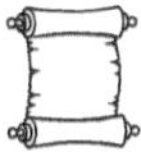

1. Jesus has many people who love His heavenly kingdom but few who are willing to carry His cross. He has many who want comfort but few who will accept suffering. Many want to celebrate with Him, but few will fast with Him. Everyone wants to rejoice with Him, but few will suffer anything for Him. Many love Jesus as long as things go well. Many praise and bless Him as long as they're receiving comfort. But when it seems Jesus pulls back and feels far away for a while, they either start complaining or fall apart.
2. But those who love Jesus for Jesus, not for the comfort He gives, bless Him in all tribulation and heartache, just as much as in times of great comfort. Even if He never gave them comfort, they would still praise Him and give Him thanks.
3. How powerful is pure love for Jesus, love not mixed with self-love or self-interest! Are those who are always seeking comfort really anything more than hired workers? Don't they show they love themselves more than Christ when they're always thinking about their own pleasure? Where

can you find someone willing to serve God for nothing in return?

4. It's rare to find someone truly stripped of love for earthly things, someone genuinely poor in spirit and free from attachment to created things. A person could give away everything they own, and it still isn't enough. They could do great acts of self-denial, and it's still just a little. They could gain all knowledge and still be far from God. They could be on fire with devotion and still be missing the one most necessary thing. What is that one thing? Leaving yourself behind, letting go completely of self-love, and when you've done everything you know you should do, knowing you've done nothing. Not thinking of yourself as great because others do, but saying honestly with Jesus, "We are unprofitable servants." And yet, no one is richer, more powerful, or more free than the person who can let go of themselves and everything else and take the lowest place.

"Jesus has many lovers of His heavenly kingdom but few bearers of His cross." That line should stop us cold. Because most of us, if we're honest, are in the first category, not the second.

We love Jesus. We love the idea of heaven. We love worship when it's moving, prayer when it feels good, and community when it's warm and welcoming. We love Jesus when life is going well. But the cross? That's different.

À Kempis identifies a specific kind of love that fails the test: love that's really about comfort. We follow Jesus because of what we get from Him, peace, purpose, forgiveness, community, or hope. None of those things are wrong. But when they become the reason we follow Him, we've turned Jesus into a means to an end.

The test is simple: What happens when the comfort goes away? When prayer feels dry, when God seems distant, when the community disappoints, and when the blessing doesn't come? Do we keep following? Or do we quietly drift when that dark night of the soul happens?

"When it seems Jesus pulls back and feels far away for a while, they either start complaining or fall apart." That's not a description of people who don't believe. That's a description of people whose faith was built on a feeling rather than love.

Pure love for Jesus, love that isn't mixed with self-interest, is the rarest thing in the world. And it's the only kind that survived the cross. The invitation is to examine our motives honestly. Not to feel guilty but to go deeper. To love Jesus for Jesus. To follow Him, not because of what we get but because of who He is.

Try this: Be honest, are you following Jesus for Jesus or for what comes with Him? Sit with that question today.

Jesus, I have to be honest, I love the comfort more than the cross. I love you when things are going well and struggle when they're not. I follow you for what I get from you more than I follow you for you. Forgive me for that. Deepen my love. Strip away the self-interest mixed in with my devotion. I want to be the kind of person who blesses you in the hard times as freely as in the good ones, who would follow you even if you never gave me another comfortable moment. Teach me to love you for you alone. Amen.

31

No Other Way

This speech seemeth hard to many, renounce thyself, take up thy cross, and follow Jesus. But it will be much harder to hear that last word, depart from me, ye cursed, into everlasting fire.

—The Christian's Pattern, 1741

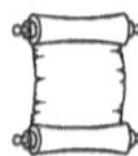

1. A lot of people find this hard to hear: "Give up everything, pick up your cross, and follow Jesus" (Matthew 16:24). But it will be a lot harder to hear this: "Depart from me, you cursed, into eternal fire" (Matthew 25:41). When Jesus comes in judgment, the sign of the cross will be in the sky (Matthew 24:30). And everyone who carried their cross faithfully will stand before Him with their heads up (1 John 2:28).
2. So why are you afraid to pick up your cross? It's the road to the kingdom (Acts 14:22). The cross is salvation. The cross is life. The cross is protection from everything that wants to destroy you. The cross is unexpected joy and real inner strength. The cross is virtue refined and holiness made complete (Galatians 6:14). There is no salvation, no hope of eternal life, outside the cross (1 Corinthians 1:18). Pick it up. Follow Jesus. That's the road to life (Matthew 16:24–25).
3. He went first. He carried His cross before you ever had to carry yours. He died on it, for you, so that you could bear yours and be joined to Him in His death (Hebrews 12:2). Die with Him, and you'll live with Him (Romans 6:8). Share His suffering and you'll share His glory (2 Timothy

2:12). Everything depends on the cross. There is no other road to life and real inner peace (Luke 14:27).

4. Go anywhere you want. Look everywhere you want. You won't find a better way up or a safer way through than the way of the cross (John 14:6). Pain will find you one way or another, in the body or in the soul (Acts 14:22).
5. Sometimes God will test you. Sometimes the people around you will wear you down. And sometimes you'll be your own worst burden (James 1:2–4). Nothing will get you out of it. As long as God allows it, you carry it because He's teaching you to endure and to surrender completely to Him (Hebrews 12:6). Nobody understands Christ's suffering more deeply than those who have suffered something like it themselves (Philippians 3:10).

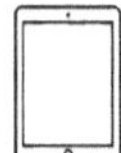

This is it. The "Royal Way of the Holy Cross." And honestly? It's not what we want to hear. We want the royal way to be about miracles, blessings, breakthroughs, and prosperity. We want the path to the kingdom to be comfortable and easy.

But à Kempis says, the royal way IS the way of the cross. There is no other way. Not alongside the cross. Not after avoiding the cross. The cross is salvation. The cross is life. The cross is joy. The cross isn't an obstacle to life; it's the way to life.

And notice how Jesus leads; He went before you. He didn't point at the cross from a safe distance. He carried it first. He died on it first. The path isn't unknown; it's been walked, and the one who walked it is waiting for you on the other side.

Try this: Name one cross you've been trying to put down. Pick it back up today, willingly and not grudgingly.

Lord Jesus, I confess I keep looking for an easier way. Forgive me. Help me see what à Kempis sees: that in the cross is everything I'm actually looking for. Salvation. Life. Peace. Not beyond it. In it. You went before me on this road. Give me the courage to follow. Amen.

32

The Cross Finds You

Truly, Jesus Christ our Lord was never one hour without suffering, as long as He lived. It behooved Christ to suffer and to rise again from the dead and so to enter into His glory. And dost thou seek any other way?

—***The Christian's Pattern, 1741***

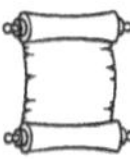

1. The cross is always there, always waiting. You can't outrun it. Wherever you go, you take yourself with you, and you'll always find yourself there too (Luke 9:23). High or low, inside or outside, whichever direction you turn, the cross is there. And patience is required everywhere you go if you want the crown that lasts (James 1:12).
2. If you carry the cross willingly, it will carry you (Matthew 11:30). If you carry it unwillingly, you make it heavier, but you still carry it. Put one cross down and another shows up, probably a harder one (Galatians 6:5).
3. Jesus was never one hour without suffering in His entire life (Isaiah 53:3). He had to suffer, die, and rise before He could enter His glory (Luke 24:26). That was His path. So, what makes you think yours will look different? His whole life was a cross, and you're still looking for comfort and ease (Philippians 2:8)?
4. None of this comes naturally. Nobody naturally loves the cross, keeps their desires in check, turns down recognition, accepts insults with a smile, denies themselves, finds joy in being overlooked, or welcomes loss and adversity (1 Corinthians 9:27). On your own, you can't do any of it (John 15:5). But trust the Lord and strength comes from above,

and the world, the flesh, and the enemy lose their grip on you (Philippians 4:13). You won't even fear the devil if you're standing in faith with the cross of Christ (Ephesians 6:16).

5. So, get ready. Steel yourself like a faithful servant of Christ to carry whatever cross He gives you (2 Timothy 2:3). Hard things are coming; wherever you are, they'll find you. Drink from the Lord's cup gladly if you want to be His friend (Matthew 20:22). As for comfort, leave that entirely to God. Let Him decide what you get and when.

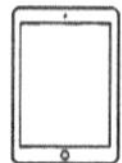

"Wherever you go, you carry yourself with you." That's the line that stops me cold. We think the cross is a circumstance, a difficult season, a hard relationship, a painful loss. Something external that will eventually pass. But à Kempis says, the cross follows you because you bring it with you. The problem isn't out there. It's in here. You can change jobs, change cities, and change relationships and still find the same cross waiting on the other side because you brought it along.

But then passage 2 turns everything around; "If you bear the cross willingly, it will bear you." You don't get to choose whether you carry it. That's already decided. What you choose is whether you carry it willingly, and that choice changes everything. The unwilling cross crushes you. The willing cross holds you up.

Try this: Identify one hardship in your life right now. Receive it as given, not just endured. See if anything shifts.

Lord, I've been trying to outrun the cross. I keep thinking if I just rearrange the circumstances, I'll find relief. Forgive me for that. Teach me that the cross finds me because I carry it and that the only way forward is through. Give me the grace to bear it willingly today, trusting that if I do, it will bear me. Amen.

33

The Dying Life

Prepare thyself for suffering and esteem hardships as thy greatest comfort. For the sufferings of this present time are not worthy to be compared to the glory that shall be revealed.

—The Christian's Pattern, 1741

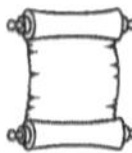

1. Get ready for suffering, and learn to see it as one of your greatest gifts. The pain of this present life doesn't come close to the glory that's coming, even if you had to bear all of it alone (Romans 8:18). When hardship starts to feel like something you can embrace for Christ's sake, you've found something rare, a kind of paradise right here on earth (James 1:2). But as long as suffering feels like something to escape, you'll be restless and troubled, and the very things you're running from will keep following you (2 Corinthians 4:17).
2. Even Paul, who was caught up to the third heaven, wasn't exempt from suffering (2 Corinthians 12:2–7). Jesus Himself said, "I will show him how much he must suffer for my name" (Acts 9:16). The conclusion is unavoidable: if you want to love Jesus and keep following Him, suffering comes with it (Colossians 1:24).
3. What an honor it would be to suffer something for Jesus' name. What joy it would bring to His people. What an encouragement to everyone watching (Acts 5:41). Everyone applauds patience; almost nobody actually practices it (James 1:3–4). Be willing to endure a little for Christ, for

plenty of people endure far worse for things that don't matter (1 Corinthians 9:25).

4. Here's the truth you have to sit with: you are called to lead a dying life (Galatians 2:20). The more you die to yourself, the more alive you become to God. Nobody gets to the things of heaven without going through the dying first (Acts 14:22).
5. If you could choose, and in a sense you can, choose suffering for Christ over comfort without Him. It's what makes you like Him. It's what made every saint before you who they were (Romans 8:17). Real spiritual growth doesn't happen in the easy seasons. It happens in the hard ones (2 Corinthians 12:9–10).
6. If there was a better path to salvation than the cross, Jesus would have shown us. He would have taken it Himself. Instead, He looked at everyone who wanted to follow Him and said plainly, "Whoever wants to come after me must deny themselves, take up their cross, and follow me" (Matthew 16:24). So, when everything has been read and considered, here's the bottom line: the road to God's kingdom runs through hard times (Acts 14:22).

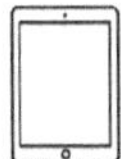

At a clergy away day, keynote speaker Dr. Peter Bellini of United Theological Seminary made a statement that shook the room: "Christianity without the Cross is satanic."[1]

Stunned silence. But he's right. When Jesus told His disciples He must go to Jerusalem to suffer and die, Peter rebuked Him, "Never, Lord!" And Jesus' response? "Get behind me, Satan" (Matthew 16:22–23). Peter was offering Jesus a Christianity without the cross. Jesus called it satanic because that's exactly what it is. It's the enemy's oldest strategy: all blessing, no cross. All comfort, no suffering. All crown, no crucifixion.

1. Dr. Peter J. Bellini, speaker at Belle Isle Methodist Church, Orlando, FL. October 9, 2024.

We've got entire movements peddling that today. Prosperity gospel. Therapeutic deism. Self-help spirituality dressed in Jesus-language. But à Kempis, and Jesus, say the same thing: There is no other way. The royal way IS the way of the cross.

Martin Luther said it best: "The cross alone is our theology." Not one option among many. The only way.

Try this: What are you avoiding that you already know God is asking of you? Take one step toward it today.

Lord Jesus, I confess I've been looking for an easier way. I want the kingdom without the cross, the crown without suffering, and the glory without pain. Forgive me. Help me embrace the royal way rather than a path that doesn't exist. Give me strength from heaven to bear what I can't bear alone. Work in me until tribulations become sweet for your sake. Help me lead a dying life, dying to myself so I can truly live to you. Through many tribulations, bring me into your kingdom. Amen.

THE CHRISTIAN'S PATTERN – BOOK THREE

ON INWARD CONSOLATION

34

Hearing God's Voice

I will hear what the Lord God will speak in me.

—The Christian's Pattern, 1741

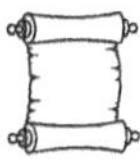

1. **Christian:** I will listen to what the Lord God speaks within me (Psalm 85:8). Blessed is the soul that hears the Lord speaking within and receives His words of comfort (Luke 10:39). Blessed are those ears that receive God's whisper and don't listen to the world's whispers (Matthew 13:16). Blessed indeed are those ears that don't listen to external voices but to the truth which teaches inwardly (John 6:45). Blessed are the eyes which are closed to external things but open to internal ones (Matthew 6:22). Blessed are they that make time to be with God and free themselves from all worldly distractions (Psalm 46:10).
2. Consider these things, my soul, and close the door on your worldly desires that you may hear what the Lord God speaks in you (Habakkuk 2:20).
   Christ: I am your peace, your life, and your salvation (John 14:27). Stay with me, and you'll find peace (John 15:4). Leave all passing things and seek things everlasting (Colossians 3:1–2). What are all earthly things but traps? And what good are all created things if the Creator abandons you (Ecclesiastes 1:2)? Leave behind, therefore, all earthly things, and work to please your Creator and be faithful to Him that you may attain true happiness (Matthew 6:33).

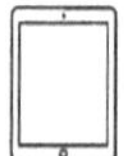

Book Three shifts into an intimate dialogue format—a conversation between Christ and the Christian soul. In these chapters, we hear the believer speaking to God and God responding, creating a beautiful model of the interior life and communion with Christ.

"I will listen to what the Lord God speaks within me." That's the posture Book Three begins with—a soul deliberately positioning itself to hear God's voice. Not straining to hear. Not demanding God speak. Just... listening.

The series of Beatitudes is beautiful: Blessed are those who hear the Lord speaking within. Blessed are the ears that receive God's whisper instead of the world's whispers. Blessed are those who listen to truth, teaching inwardly. Blessed are eyes closed to external distractions but open to internal realities. Blessed are those who make space for God.

We live in the noisiest age in human history. Our ears are bombarded with the world's whispers and shouts, voices telling us what to want, who to be, and how to live. And in all that noise, God's voice gets drowned out, not because He's not speaking but because we're not listening.

"Consider these things, my soul, and close the door on your worldly desires that you may hear what the Lord God speaks in you." Close the door. Turn off the noise. Create space. Be still. Then comes Christ's response; "I am your peace, your life, and your salvation." That's what we're listening for, not information but a *Person*. Not instructions but intimacy.

Try this: Set a timer for five minutes. Sit in silence. No agenda, just listen. See what happens.

Lord, I want to hear your voice. But I'm surrounded by noise, the world's chatter, my own desires, endless distractions. Teach me to close the door on all that and create space to hear you. Help me understand that you don't just give me peace; you ARE my peace. You're not just offering life; you ARE my life. Forgive me for chasing passing things as if they could satisfy. Show me that everything I grab for is a trap if I don't have you. In the silence, speak. In the stillness, show yourself. Amen.

35

Truth Without Words

Speak, Lord, for thy servant heareth.

—The Christian's Pattern, 1741

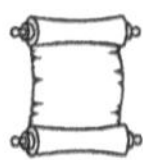

1. **Christian:** Speak, Lord, your servant is listening (1 Samuel 3:9). I am your servant; give me understanding so I may know your testimonies (Psalm 119:125). Turn my heart toward your words (Psalm 119:36). Let your words fall like dew (Deuteronomy 32:2). The children of Israel once said to Moses, "Speak to us, and we will hear; don't let the Lord speak to us, or we'll die" (Exodus 20:19). No, Lord, not that, I beg you. But rather, with the Prophet Samuel, I humbly and earnestly ask, "Speak, Lord, your servant is listening" (1 Samuel 3:9). Don't let Moses speak to me, nor any of the prophets. But you speak, Lord God; you alone without them can perfectly instruct me, but they without you accomplish nothing (John 6:63).
2. They may speak words, but they cannot give the Spirit (2 Corinthians 3:6). They speak well, but if you're silent, they don't set the heart on fire (Luke 24:32). They teach the letter, but you open the meaning (2 Corinthians 3:6). They reveal mysteries, but you unlock their meaning (Daniel 2:22). They declare your commandments, but you help us fulfill them (Philippians 2:13). They show the way, but you give the strength to walk in it (Isaiah 40:29). They work only outwardly, but you instruct and enlighten the heart (Ephesians 1:18). They water, but you give the

increase (1 Corinthians 3:6–7). Their words make noise, but you give understanding (Proverbs 2:6).

3. So don't let Moses speak to me, but you, my Lord God, speak the everlasting truth, or I might die spiritually and prove unfaithful if I'm only warned outwardly and not set on fire within (Romans 2:13). Don't let me hear the word but not do it, know it but not love it, or believe it but not obey it, or it will condemn me (James 1:22). Speak, therefore, Lord, your servant is listening, for you have the words of eternal life (John 6:68). Speak to me, to the comfort of my soul, to the transformation of my whole life, and to your praise, glory, and everlasting honor (Psalm 119:107).

"Speak, Lord, your servant is listening." That's Samuel's response when God called him in the night (1 Samuel 3:9). And it's the prayer that opens this chapter, the posture of a soul ready to hear God speak without intermediaries.

The contrast with Israel at Sinai is striking. When God came down on the mountain, the people were terrified and said to Moses, "Speak to us, and we will hear; don't let the Lord speak to us, or we'll die." They wanted a mediator. A buffer. But à Kempis is saying, Not me. I want God to speak directly. It's not arrogance; it's hunger.

The series of contrasts in passage 2 is brilliant. They teach the letter, but YOU open the meaning. They declare your commandments, but YOU help us fulfill them. They show the way, but YOU give us strength to walk in it. Human teachers are necessary but not sufficient. All the teaching in the world won't transform you if God doesn't speak it into your heart.

"Don't let me hear the word but not do it, know it but not love it, or believe it but not obey it, or it will condemn me." Knowledge without obedience and belief without transformation is the danger. And that's why we need God to speak, not just through teachers but *to* us.

Try this: Before your next Bible study or podcast, ask God to speak to you directly. Then actually wait.

Lord, I don't want secondhand knowledge of you. I want YOU to speak. Thank you for teachers, preachers, mentors, and all those who water the seed, but without you making it grow, all their words are just noise. They can teach the letter, but only you can open up the meaning. They can tell me your commandments, but only you can help me actually follow them. Forgive me for being satisfied with external warning without internal transformation. Speak to me on the inside. Set my heart on fire. Give me not just information but transformation. Speak, Lord, I'm listening. You have the words of eternal life. Amen.

36

Why Many Don't Listen

Many words satisfy not the soul, but a good life refresheth the mind.

—*The Christian's Pattern, 1741*

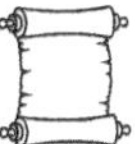

1. **Christ:** My child, hear my words—words of the greatest sweetness, surpassing all the knowledge of the philosophers and wise men of this world (1 Corinthians 1:25). My words are spirit and life, beyond human understanding (John 6:63). Listen to them in silence and receive them with all humility and great affection (James 1:19, 21).
   Christian: Blessed is the one you instruct, Lord, and teach your law so you may give them rest from evil days and they won't be destroyed upon the earth (Psalm 94:12–13).
2. **Christ:** I have taught the prophets from the beginning and continue, even today, to speak to everyone. But many are hardened and deaf to my speech (Isaiah 6:9–10). Most people would rather listen to the world than to God and more readily follow the desires of the flesh than the will of God (Romans 8:5–7). The world promises temporary and trivial things and is eagerly served. I promise high and eternal things, and people's hearts remain unmoved. Who serves and obeys me as carefully as people serve the world and its rulers (Luke 16:8)? You should be ashamed, lazy and complaining servant, that they are more eager for destruction than you are for life (Proverbs 1:32). They rejoice more in vanity than you do in the truth (Psalm 4:2).
3. And yet they are often disappointed in their hopes. But my promise never deceives nor sends anyone who trusts in me away empty-handed (Hebrews 10:23). What I have promised I will give. I will fulfill what I have said to those

who remain faithful to my love until the end (Revelation 2:10). Write my words in your heart and think carefully about them, for they will be very necessary in the time of temptation (Psalm 119:11).

4. What you don't understand when you read, you'll know when I visit you (1 Peter 2:12). I visit my elect two ways: with temptation and with comfort (James 1:12; 2 Corinthians 1:3–4). And every day I teach them two lessons: one correcting their sins and another encouraging them to grow in virtue (2 Timothy 3:16). Those who have my words and despise them will be judged on the last day (John 12:48).
   Christian: Lord my God, you are to me everything that is good. Who am I to dare speak to you? I am your poorest servant and completely insignificant. Yet remember, Lord, that I am nothing, have nothing, and can do nothing (John 15:5). You alone are good, just, and holy. You send only the proud away empty (Luke 1:53). Remember your mercies and fill my heart with your grace.

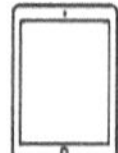

"You should be ashamed, lazy and complaining servant, that they are more eager for destruction than you are for life." Ouch. That stings. But it's true. People serve the world with more passion, more dedication, and more sacrifice than they serve God. The world promises "temporary and trivial things," and people pursue them with great eagerness. God promises "high and eternal things," and our hearts are "unmoved."

But here's what Christ says: "My promise never deceives, nor sends anyone away empty-handed who trusts in me." The world overpromises and underdelivers. But God keeps His promises. Every. Single. Time.

The instruction in passage 3 is crucial: "Write my words in your heart and think carefully about them, for they will be very necessary in the time of temptation." You need God's word stored up, memorized, internalized, not just for information but for *transformation.*

When temptation comes, you won't have time to search for the right verse. You need it written on your heart.

Try this: Pick one verse today and memorize it. Not for a quiz, for the moment when you'll need it.

Lord, forgive me. I'm more excited about the world's empty promises than your eternal life. I chase temporary things with passion and eternal things with apathy. Open my deaf ears. Soften my hard heart. Help me listen to your voice more eagerly than the world's voice. Thank you that your promises never fail; what you promise, you deliver. Write your words on my heart. Help me think about them constantly. Make them essential to me when temptation comes. I admit it: I am nothing, have nothing, and can do nothing. You alone are good, just, and holy. Remember your mercy and fill my heart with your grace. Amen.

37

Walk in Truth

Walk before me in truth and always seek me with a simple heart.

—The Christian's Pattern, 1741

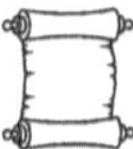

1. **Christ:** My child, walk before me in truth and always seek me with a simple heart (Genesis 17:1; Psalm 86:11). Those who walk before me in truth will be protected from evil, and the truth will deliver them from deceivers (Psalm 91:4). If the truth makes you free, you'll be free indeed (John 8:32, 36).
   Christian: Lord, what you say is true, so I pray it will be so with me. Let your truth teach me and keep me and bring me safely to a blessed end (Psalm 25:5). Let it deliver me from all unhealthy desires and disordered love, and I will walk with you in great freedom of heart (Galatians 5:1).
   Christ: I will teach you those things that are right and pleasing in my sight (Micah 6:8).
2. The truth is, you're a sinner; you're driven by emotions and weighed down by struggles you can't control (Romans 7:14–24). On your own, you're heading nowhere. You get discouraged easily, defeated easily, anxious easily, and you fall apart easily. You have nothing to brag about but plenty to be humble about, for you're much weaker than you realize (Jeremiah 17:9). So, don't be proud of anything you accomplish (Luke 17:10). Let eternal truth satisfy you above everything else. Let your own weakness keep you humble (Psalm 51:3). Fear nothing and avoid nothing so much as your own sins and destructive patterns.
3. Some people don't live honestly before me; they want to understand deep spiritual mysteries while ignoring their

> own mess and their need for salvation (Colossians 2:18). Because I resist them, they often fall into serious temptation and sin (James 4:6). Look at your own failures, how much you've messed up and how much good you've left undone (Psalm 139:23–24). But there are others who have clear minds and pure hearts, who constantly long for eternal things. They understand what the Spirit of truth is saying to them (1 Corinthians 2:10–12), and the Spirit teaches them to turn away from earthly things and love heavenly things (Colossians 3:1–2).

"Walk before me in truth and always seek me with a simple heart." Not complexity. Not sophisticated theology. Not impressive religious performance. Just truth and simplicity. "If the truth makes you free, you'll be free indeed."

But truth about us is painful. "The truth is you're a sinner; you're driven by emotions and weighed down by struggles you can't control. On your own, you're heading nowhere." That's hard to hear in a culture that tells us to "trust yourself" and "you've got this." But here's the diagnostic: Does your spiritual knowledge make you more humble or more proud? More patient with others' failures or more judgmental?

The warning against spiritual curiosity without personal holiness is sobering. "Some people don't live honestly before me. They want to understand deep spiritual mysteries while ignoring their own mess." We can be so busy trying to understand deep theology that we neglect our own souls. The goal isn't to master Scripture but to let Scripture master you.

Try this: Name one thing you know theologically but haven't practiced this week. Close the gap today.

Lord, teach me to walk honestly before you and seek you with a simple heart. I overcomplicate things. I overthink. I perform. But you're calling me to simple, honest truth. Set me free. Help me face my sins with genuine sorrow and regret. Don't let me think I'm something special because of my good works. Show me the truth about myself: I get discouraged easily, defeated easily, and anxious easily. I have nothing to brag about and many things to be ashamed of. Help me stop taking credit for anything I do. Let nothing seem great except what lasts forever. Make me fear nothing and avoid nothing, except my sins and destructive patterns. And light up my understanding so I constantly long for eternal things. Amen.

38

The Wonderful Effects of Divine Love

Love is a great thing, a great good in every wise; it alone maketh everything that is heavy light and beareth evenly all that is uneven.

—The Christian's Pattern, 1741

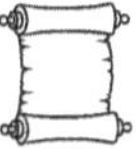

1. **Christian:** I praise you, Father in heaven, Father of my Lord, Jesus Christ, for remembering me, even though I'm unworthy. Father of mercies and God of all comfort, thank you for comforting me, even though I don't deserve it. Lord, you love my soul perfectly. When you come into my heart, everything within me comes alive with joy. You are my glory and the joy of my heart. You are my hope and my refuge when I'm in trouble.
2. But I'm still weak in love, so I need you to strengthen and comfort me. Stay close to me and show me how to follow you. Free me from sinful desires and heal my heart from all unhealthy attachments. Then, with a healed heart, I'll be ready to love deeply, strong enough to suffer, and steady enough to keep going.
3. **Christ:** Love is powerful; it makes every burden light and helps us handle life's difficulties. Love carries a burden as if it weighs nothing. It makes bitter things taste sweet. The love of Jesus drives us to do great things and constantly pushes us toward deeper maturity. Love wants to be free, not trapped by worldly attachments. Nothing is sweeter than love; nothing is stronger, higher, or better in heaven

or on earth. Love comes from God and can't rest anywhere except in God, above all created things.

4. Someone who loves soars, runs free, and celebrates, they give everything for God, who is everything, and find everything in God, from whom all good comes. They don't focus on the gifts but look beyond them to the Giver. Love often breaks through all boundaries. Love feels no burden, doesn't worry about difficulty, and attempts things beyond its strength because it believes anything is possible.
5. Love stays alert. Even when exhausted, it doesn't quit. When under pressure, it doesn't stress out. When threatened, it doesn't panic. Like a living flame, it shoots upward and breaks through every obstacle. The soul cries out to God with passionate devotion, "My God, my love, you are completely mine, and I am completely yours."
6. **Christian:** Help me love more, Lord, so I can experience deep in my soul how sweet it is to love, to melt into your love and be immersed in it. Let love consume me, lifting me beyond myself in total devotion and praise. Let me sing the song of love. Let me follow you to the heights, my beloved.
7. **Christ:** Love is quick, genuine, devoted, pleasant, and joyful. It's strong, patient, faithful, wise, enduring, courageous, and it never seeks its own interests. The moment someone becomes self-seeking, they've stopped loving. Love is careful, humble, and honest. It submits to authority and is devoted and grateful to God, always trusting and hoping in Him. A true lover willingly embraces everything hard and painful for the sake of the one they love.

This chapter reads almost like poetry because it's about the most beautiful thing in the universe: divine love. But à Kempis doesn't describe love as a warm feeling. He describes it as a force—active, powerful, transformative. Love "soars, runs free, and celebrates."

Love "carries a burden as if it weighs nothing." Love "breaks through every obstacle."

I think about the people I've known who really embodied this kind of love. They weren't perfect, but they could face hard things without complaining, serve without resentment, and love difficult people without becoming bitter. They were so filled with the love of Christ that it overflowed into everything.

The prayer in section 6 is worth praying daily. "Help me love more, Lord, so I can experience deep in my soul how sweet it is to love." We need God to help us love more. And as He does, we find that we can love in ways we never thought possible.

Try this: Ask God for more love, not as a feeling to summon but as a gift to receive. Then act like He gave it.

Lord Jesus, help me love more. Let me experience your love so deeply that it overflows into every area of my life. Teach me what it means to love the way you love, freely, sacrificially, and joyfully. Help me carry burdens without complaining, face difficulties without despairing, and serve others without seeking anything in return. When I'm weak in love, strengthen me. When my love grows cold, warm me again with your presence. Let me be so filled with your love that it becomes the defining characteristic of my life. I want to love you more than I love myself and to love others because of you. Make me a person who truly loves, not just in words but in actions and truth. In your name I pray, amen.

39

Proof of a True Lover

Love is a mighty power, a great and complete good; Love alone lightens every burden and makes the rough places smooth.

—The Christian's Pattern, 1741

1. **Christ:** My child, you're not yet a strong and wise lover.
   Christian: Why not, Lord?
   Christ: Because you quit your commitments when you face even small difficulties, and you're too quick to look for comfort. A strong lover stands firm when tempted and doesn't fall for the enemy's lies. I'm just as much for him in hard times as I am in good times.
2. A wise lover doesn't focus so much on the gift as on the love of the one giving it. He values their love more than what's given, and he values me above all gifts. A mature lover doesn't stop at the gift but looks to me, the one who gives every gift.
3. Know that your enemy is always working to kill your desire for good and distract you from spiritual growth. Specifically, he tries to pull you away from thinking about my suffering, being aware of your own sins, guarding your heart carefully, and being committed to grow in holiness. He fills your mind with evil thoughts, trying to discourage and terrify you—anything to drive you away from prayer and from reading Scripture. Prayer threatens him, and if he could, he would stop you from receiving communion. Don't trust him or listen to him, even though he's constantly setting traps for you. When he suggests evil thoughts to you, tell him, "Get away from me, evil spirit! You should be ashamed, you wretched thing! You're com-

pletely disgusting, bringing such filth to my mind. Leave me alone, you liar! You'll get nothing from me. Jesus will be with me as a mighty warrior, and you'll be left standing there defeated" (Psalm 27:1). "The Lord is my light and my salvation; whom should I fear? Even if armies surround me, my heart won't be afraid. The Lord is my helper and my redeemer" (Psalm 27:1, 3, 14).

This chapter asks a piercing question: Are we true lovers of God, or are we just spiritual consumers? The difference is a spiritual consumer loves God for the benefits, while a true lover loves God for who He is.

Christ challenges the Christian here: "You quit your commitments when you face even small difficulties, and you're too quick to look for comfort." A true lover "stands firm when tempted" and is just as devoted in hard times as in good times. We keep showing up. We keep praying even when prayer feels dry. We keep serving even when we're tired.

The second mark of a true lover is even more challenging: focusing on the Giver rather than the gifts. It's so easy to love God for what He gives us, like blessings, answered prayers, and good feelings in worship. But do we love Him when those things aren't there? Do we love Him simply because He is God and worthy of our love?

The section on spiritual warfare is a reminder we need: the devil actively works to distract us from spiritual growth. He doesn't want us praying, reading Scripture, or receiving communion. The remedy? Don't engage. Don't debate. Call on Jesus' name and redirect your attention back to God.

Try this: The next time the enemy throws a dark thought at you, name it out loud and refuse it. Don't negotiate.

Lord Jesus, make me a true lover, one who loves you for who you are not just for what you give me. Forgive me for giving up too easily when things get hard. Strengthen my commitment to keep praying when prayer feels dry, keep reading when Scripture seems boring, keep serving when I'm tired. Let me seek your face, not just your hand. Protect me from the enemy's schemes. When he fills my mind with discouraging thoughts, help me recognize his lies and turn immediately back to you. You are my light, my salvation, my helper, and my redeemer. Amen.

40

Grace Must Be Guarded by Humility

Without me, thou canst do nothing.

—*The Christian's Pattern, 1741*

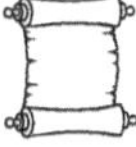

1. **Christ:** Think about this: Imagine how desperate you'd be without my grace. You don't control your spiritual life. It belongs to God; He gives grace and comfort when He wants, how much He wants, and to whomever He wants. It all depends on what pleases Him, nothing more. New believers who are still learning can easily be deceived and led astray unless they get advice from wise, experienced people.
2. And if they insist on trusting their own judgment instead of listening to those with more experience, things will end badly for them. People who think they have it all figured out rarely humble themselves enough to be guided by others.
3. **Christian:** Can I even speak to you, Lord, when I'm just dust and ashes? If I think too highly of myself, you oppose me, and my sins prove you're right. But if I humble myself and admit I'm nothing, if I let go of all pride and recognize what I really am, just dust, then your grace comes to me, and your light reaches my heart.
4. Your love does this, freely protecting me and helping me in so many ways. It keeps me from serious dangers and rescues me from countless problems. By loving myself in unhealthy ways, I lost myself. But by seeking only you

and loving you purely, I found both myself and you. And through that love, I've completely surrendered myself. For you, blessed Lord, treat me far better than I deserve or could ever hope for or ask.

5. Blessed are you, my God! Even though I don't deserve any blessings, your generosity and endless goodness never stop doing good, even to ungrateful people and those who have walked away from you. Bring us back to you, Lord, so we can be thankful, humble, and holy because you are our power, our strength, and our salvation.

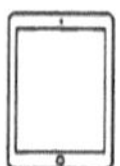

This chapter presents one of Christianity's most beautiful paradoxes: The lower we go in humility, the higher we rise in grace.

"If I humble myself and admit I'm nothing, if I let go of all pride and recognize what I really am, just dust, then your grace comes to me." This isn't self-loathing or false modesty. It's honest self-assessment before a holy God. It's recognizing that apart from Christ, we can do nothing (John 15:5).

The chapter warns against two specific dangers: spiritual pride (thinking we've "arrived") and forgetting our dependence on God. "If I'm on my own, I'm nothing but weak. But when you turn your attention to me, I'm suddenly strong." Every spiritual strength we have is a gift. Every victory is God's doing. Every bit of growth is His grace at work.

Try this: Take credit for nothing good today. Every time something goes right, trace it back to God.

Lord, teach me true humility, not self-hatred but honest self-assessment before you. Show me who I really am: created in your image and deeply loved but completely dependent on your grace for everything good in my life. Protect me from spiritual pride. When I start thinking I've got this Christian life figured out, remind me that I'm still learning. Help me stay teachable, willing to listen to wise counsel, and humble enough to admit when I'm wrong. Thank you that when I come low before you, you lift me up. Keep me aware of my daily, moment-by-moment need for you. Bring me back to you whenever I drift. Make me thankful, humble, and holy. In Jesus' name, amen.

41

Make God Your Final Goal

Son, I ought to be your chief and last end if you desire to be truly blessed. By this intention, your affection shall be purified, which is often inordinately bent down to itself and unto creatures.

—*The Christian's Pattern, 1741*

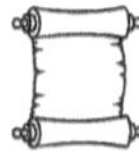

1. **Christ:** My child, I should be your chief and ultimate goal if you want to be truly blessed. When you make me your final aim, your desires get purified because they're constantly being bent downward toward yourself and toward created things. Refer everything back to me, for I am the one who gave it all. Think of everything as flowing from the highest good, and therefore, everything should be returned to me, its original source.
2. Out of me, like a living fountain, both the small and the great, the poor and the rich, draw the water of life. Those who serve me freely and willingly will receive grace upon grace. But anyone who seeks glory outside of me or finds delight in anything that doesn't lead back to me won't find true joy or inner freedom. They'll be weighed down and tangled up in countless ways. So don't take credit for anything good. Don't attribute goodness to any person. Give everything to God, without whom no one has anything. I have given everything, and I require that all things be returned to me with genuine thanksgiving.
3. This is the truth that defeats empty pride. When heavenly grace and true love come in, envy and inner conflict disappear because there's no room left for self-love. Divine love

conquers everything and expands all the powers of the soul. If you are truly wise, you will find your joy and hope in me alone. For no one is good but God, who is to be praised above all things and blessed in all things.

"I should be your chief and ultimate goal if you want to be truly blessed." We set a lot of goals, career goals, financial goals, health goals, relationship goals. We have five-year plans and bucket lists and vision boards. And there's nothing wrong with any of that. But this chapter asks a deeper question: What is your final goal? What is the thing everything else is moving toward? What are you ultimately living for?

À Kempis puts it plainly: If you want to be truly blessed, God has to be the answer to that question. Not a means to an end, not "I want God's blessing so I can achieve my goals," but the end itself. The problem is that our desires constantly bend downward. We start out wanting God, but slowly, we find ourselves wanting what God can give us more than we want God Himself.

The solution is to refer everything back to God. Every gift, every blessing, every good thing, trace it back to the source and return thanks to the one who gave it. This isn't just gratitude as a spiritual discipline. It's a reorientation of the whole self toward the only end that can truly satisfy.

Try this: Identify one thing you're pursuing that's a means to something else. Ask if God Himself is the end.

Lord, I confess that my desires bend downward toward comfort, recognition, security, and success more often than they bend toward you. I've been treating you as a means to an end rather than the end itself. Forgive me for that. Recalibrate my soul. Make yourself my chief and final goal, the thing everything else flows toward and returns to. When I receive good things, help me trace them back to you and give thanks. When I'm tempted to take credit, remind me that I have nothing that didn't come from you. Make me wise enough to find my joy and my hope in you alone. Amen.

42

The Sweetness of Serving God

O how great is the abundance of thy goodness, O Lord, which thou hast laid up for them that fear thee! But what art thou to them that love thee and serve thee with their whole heart? Truly unspeakable is the sweetness of contemplating thee.

—The Christian's Pattern, 1741

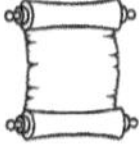

1. **Christian:** Lord, let me speak; I can't stay silent. O how great is the abundance of your goodness, which you've stored up for those who fear you! But what are you to those who love you? What are you to those who serve you with everything they have? The sweetness of knowing you, which you pour out on those who love you, is beyond words. This is how you've shown me the sweetness of your love: When I didn't exist, you made me. When I wandered far away from you, you brought me back so I could serve you, and you commanded me to love you.
2. O fountain of everlasting love, what can I say about you? How can I forget you, when you remembered me even when I had wasted away and perished? You've shown mercy to your servant far beyond anything I expected. You've shown favor and friendship far beyond anything I deserved. What can I give you in return? Is it really so much that I should serve you when everything that exists is bound to serve you? It shouldn't seem like much that I serve you. What seems like much to me is this: that you would accept someone as poor and unworthy as me into your service and place me alongside your beloved servants.
3. Everything I have is yours, and with it I serve you. And yet, remarkably, you serve me more than I serve you. Heaven

and earth, which you created for the service of humanity, are ready at hand and do whatever you command. Beyond that, you appointed angels to serve people. But most amazing of all, you yourself have chosen to serve us, and you have promised to give yourself to us.

4. What can I give you for all these thousands of blessings? I wish I could serve you every day of my life! I wish I could offer you even one day of truly worthy service! You deserve all service, all honor, and eternal praise. You are my Lord, and I am your servant, bound to serve you with everything I have, and I should never grow tired of praising you. This is my desire. Whatever I lack, please supply.

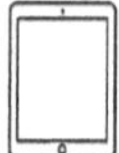

This chapter is a love song, and it gets at something that gets lost in the more disciplined, duty-focused chapters: Serving God isn't just the right thing to do; it's the sweetest thing there is. We often talk about the Christian life in terms of obligation. We *should* pray. We *should* read Scripture. We *should* serve. And all of that is true. But à Kempis is describing something different—the experience of someone who has tasted God's goodness so deeply that serving Him feels like the greatest privilege imaginable.

"When I didn't exist, you made me. When I wandered far away, you brought me back." That's the foundation. Before we ever sought God, He was seeking us. Before we ever loved Him, He loved us. The Christian life isn't us climbing up to God; it's responding to a God who came down to us. And then this stunning reversal, "You serve me more than I serve you." God, the Creator of everything, stoops down to serve His creatures.

When we really understand that, the question stops being "How much do I have to do for God?" and starts being "How could I ever do enough?" Not out of guilt but out of gratitude. Not obligation but joy. That's the sweetness à Kempis is describing. And it's available to anyone who stops treating God as a duty and starts knowing Him as a friend.

Try this: Do one thing in service to God today purely for the joy of it, not out of duty. Notice the difference.

Lord, forgive me for treating your service as an obligation rather than a privilege. I've been going through the motions, doing what I'm supposed to do without really tasting the sweetness of knowing you. Open my eyes to see what you've actually done for me. You made me, you found me when I was lost, you serve me more than I serve you, and you've promised to give yourself to me. That's overwhelming. That's more than I know what to do with. Stir up genuine love in my heart, not just duty, not just discipline, but real delight in you. Make your service sweet to me. And whatever I lack to love you well, supply it yourself. Amen.

43

The Desires of Our Hearts Must Be Examined

Son, thou must learn in many things to deny thy self, if thou wilt keep peace and concord with others.

—*The Christian's Pattern, 1741*

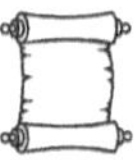

1. **Christ:** My child, you still have many things to learn which you haven't fully grasped yet.
   Christian: What are those things, Lord?
   Christ: That you align your desires completely with what pleases me and that you stop being self-focused and become instead a wholehearted follower of my will. Your desires often fire you up and push you forward intensely. But think carefully about whether you're actually motivated by my honor or by your own self-interest. If I'm the reason for your actions, you'll be content with however things turn out. But if there's any self-seeking hiding in you, that's what's actually holding you back and weighing you down.

2. Don't get too attached to your plans without asking me first. Otherwise, you might regret it later and end up hating what you previously wanted so badly. Don't act on every impulse that feels right, and don't avoid every uncomfortable feeling. Use self-control even when you're pursuing good desires and goals. Otherwise, you might become distracted by giving in to every impulse, damage your witness through lack of discipline, or get into serious trouble. But forcefully resist your sinful desires and ignore

what your body craves or avoids. Instead, make your body submit to your spirit (1 Corinthians 9:27).

3. You're just dust so learn obedience. You're nothing but dirt so learn to humble yourself before others. Break your stubborn will and surrender completely. Fight passionately against your own selfishness, and don't let pride control you. Be so humble, so childlike, that you can bear being treated as nothing.
4. I've shown you mercy because your soul is precious to me. I did this so you would understand my love and stay grateful for my blessings. And so that you would constantly practice genuine submission and humility and patiently bear being looked down on.

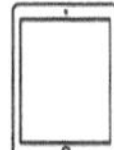

This is one of the most searching chapters in the entire book. It asks the question we often avoid: *Why am I really doing this?* Christ challenges the Christian, "Think carefully whether you're actually motivated by my honor or by your own self-interest." How many times have we done good things for mixed motives, partly for God's glory but also partly for recognition, approval, or personal satisfaction?

The chapter gives us three diagnostic questions: Am I content with however things turn out? Am I willing to wait and seek guidance? And can I handle being humbled? "Be so humble, so childlike, that you can bear being treated as nothing." This is hard. If my motivation is pure love for God, I can handle criticism and rejection. But if I'm motivated by pride, those things will devastate me.

There's a difference between worldly ambition and a desire to make a difference for the kingdom. I'll never forget what my first district superintendent told me: "Son, there are pastors who are chasing steeples and those who carry the cross." My response when people compliment the sermon is always the same: "I'm glad it mattered."

Not "I'm glad you liked it," which makes it about me, but "I'm glad it mattered," which keeps the focus on impact rather than applause.

Try this: Before your next good deed, check your motive. Then, do it anyway, and ask God to purify what's mixed.

Lord Jesus, search my heart and examine my motives. Show me where I'm serving you for my own glory rather than yours. Reveal where I'm seeking recognition and approval rather than simply obeying you. Give me courage to wait and seek your guidance before acting on my desires, even my good desires. Help me distinguish what seems good from what actually is good. Break my stubborn will. Teach me genuine humility, the kind that doesn't think of itself at all. Keep transforming me into someone who loves you purely, serves you faithfully, and glorifies you in everything. Amen.

44

Considering God's Secret Judgments

Thy judgments are right, O Lord, and thy judgment is according to truth.

—The Christian's Pattern, 1741

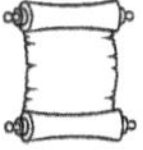

1. **Christian:** Your judgments thunder over me, Lord. You shake me to my core with fear and trembling, and I'm terrified deep in my soul (Psalm 6:2–3). I'm stunned when I think that even the heavens aren't pure in your sight (Job 15:15). If you found evil in angels and didn't spare them, what will become of me (2 Peter 2:4)? Stars fell from heaven, and who am I, just dust, to be proud (Revelation 12:4)?
2. There's no holiness if you, Lord, withdraw your hand. No wisdom helps if you stop guiding. No strength holds up if you stop defending. No purity stays safe if you don't protect it. If we're left alone, we sink and die. But when you come to us, we're lifted up and live. We're unstable, but you make us steady. We grow cold, but you set us on fire with love.
3. How humbly I should think of myself! How little should I think of any good in me! Lord, how deeply I should humble myself before your mysterious judgments, where I find myself to be nothing, a nothing, a complete nothing! O, immeasurable weight! O, unpassable sea where I find myself to be nothing, absolutely nothing! Where can pride hide then? Where's my confidence in my own goodness? All self-glory disappears in the depths of your judgment over me.
4. What is any human in your sight (Isaiah 40:6)? Can the clay boast against the one who formed it (Romans 9:21)?

> How can someone be proud when their heart is truly given to God? All the world can't lift up someone truth has humbled. Someone who puts all their hope in God won't be swayed by others' praise. For even those who praise me are nothing; they'll pass away like their words. But the truth of the Lord remains forever (Psalm 117:2).

This chapter might be the most intense in the entire book. It's a meditation on the absolute holiness of God and our utter unworthiness before Him. For modern readers, especially those raised on comfortable Christianity, this can feel jarring. But here's what à Kempis is getting at: We need a proper sense of God's holiness before we can truly understand grace.

If we think we're pretty good people who just need a little help from God, we'll never grasp the magnitude of what Christ did for us on the cross. But when we see ourselves as the chapter describes—nothing, absolutely nothing—then grace becomes amazing.

The ending is beautiful. "All the world can't lift up someone truth has humbled." When we've truly grasped how unworthy we are, other people's praise doesn't go to our heads. And when we've truly grasped how much God loves us, other people's criticism doesn't crush us. The goal isn't to grovel in perpetual self-loathing. The goal is to be so honest about our weakness that we rely completely on God's strength.

Try this: Stop explaining why you deserve more than you have. Spend that energy thanking God for what you do.

Lord, give me a proper sense of your holiness and my unworthiness. Help me see myself clearly, not through the lens of pride or the lens of despair but through the lens of truth. Without you, I am nothing. Every good thing in my life comes from you. Every strength I have is your gift. Kill my pride. Show me that all my self-glorying is empty. And yet, help me remember that while I am nothing in myself, I am precious in your sight. You who are always the same establish me when I am unstable, set me on fire when I grow cold, and raise me up when I sink. Be my holiness, my wisdom, and my strength. Let my entire hope rest in you alone. In Jesus' name, amen.

45

How to Approach Our Desires

Lord, if this pleases thee, so be it. Lord, if it be to thine honor, in thy name let this be done.

—*The Christian's Pattern, 1741*

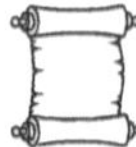

1. **Christ:** My child, say this in every situation, "Lord, if this pleases you, make it happen. Lord, if it brings you honor, do this in your name. Lord, if you see that this is good for me and know it will help me, then let me use this for your honor. But if you know this will harm me and isn't good for my soul, take this desire away from me." Not every desire comes from the Holy Spirit, even though it may seem right and good to us. It's hard to tell whether a good spirit or an evil spirit is driving a particular desire or whether we're simply being driven by our own ego. Many people end up deceived by what initially seemed to be a good spirit.
2. Therefore, whatever you desire should be asked for with reverence for God and a humble heart. And above all, you should surrender completely and say, "Lord, you know what's best. Do whatever you want. Give what you want, how much you want, and when you want. Deal with me however you think best and do whatever pleases you most and brings you the most honor. Put me wherever you want, and handle everything in my life according to your will. I'm in your hands. Turn me whichever way you want. I'm your servant, ready for anything. I don't want to live for myself but for you. Help me do this well!"
3. Give me your grace, gracious Jesus, so it will be with me, work in me, and stay with me to the end. Help me always

want and choose what pleases you most and you like best. Let your will be mine and let my will always follow yours and perfectly align with it. Make my will and your will completely one so I only want what you want and only refuse what you refuse.

4. Help me die to everything in the world and for your sake, be okay with being looked down on and unknown in this world. Help me find rest in you above everything else and calm my heart in you. You are the true peace of the heart. You are the only rest. Without you, everything is troubling and restless. In this peace, in you, the one eternal good, let me rest. Amen.

This chapter gives us one of the most practical and transformative prayers in the entire book. It's a template for how to bring every desire to God, big or small, spiritual or mundane. The key phrase is repeated throughout, "Lord, if it pleases you..."

Notice what this prayer does. First, it acknowledges that we don't always know what's best. "Not every desire comes from the Holy Spirit, even though it may seem right and good to us." We can be sincere and still be sincerely wrong. We need God's wisdom, not just our own discernment. Second, it submits every desire to God's will. "But if you know this will harm me, take this desire away from me." This is scary to pray. But it's also deeply freeing because it means we can trust that whatever we receive is what's ultimately best for us.

This is the prayer Jesus prayed in Gethsemane: "Not my will, but yours be done" (Luke 22:42). He wanted desperately to avoid the cross, but He submitted that desire to the Father's greater purpose. The beautiful ending captures what this surrender leads to: "You are the true peace of the heart. You are the only rest. Without you, everything is troubling and restless."

Try this: Bring one specific desire to God today, not to get it but to surrender it. Let Him decide.

Lord, teach me to bring every desire to you with an open hand, ready to receive if you give and ready to release if you withhold. Give me wisdom to discern which desires come from you and which come from my flesh. When I want something badly, help me pray, "Lord, if this is for your glory and my good, give it. If not, take the desire away." Give me the courage to mean those words. Let your will be mine. I am in your hands. I am your servant. When I surrender my desires to you, give me your peace. In Jesus' name, amen.

46

True Comfort Is to Be Found in God Alone

Whatsoever I can desire or imagine for my comfort, I look not for it here but hereafter. For if I should alone have all the comforts of the world, it is certain they could not last long.

—*The Christian's Pattern, 1741*

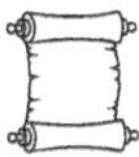

1. **Christian:** My soul, you can't find full comfort or complete joy in anything except God, who comforts the poor and helps the humble.
2. **Christ:** My child, if you want to follow me, you need this mindset: You must be as willing to suffer as to celebrate. You must be as willing to be poor and in need as to be comfortable and wealthy.
3. **Christian:** Lord, I'll willingly suffer for you whatever you allow to happen to me. I'll accept from you both good and bad, sweet and bitter, joyful and painful, and thank you for everything that happens to me. Keep me from sin, and I won't fear death or hell. As long as you don't reject me forever or erase me from the book of life, whatever trouble comes won't really harm me.
4. Be patient, my soul. Wait for God's promise, and you'll have plenty of everything good. Use earthly things but want eternal things. You can never be satisfied with anything earthly because you weren't created to find ultimate satisfaction in it. Even if you had everything created, you still wouldn't be happy or blessed. Your complete happiness is found only in God, who created everything. All human comfort is empty and temporary. Blessed and genuine

> is the comfort that comes from truth within. "Let this comfort me: that I'm willing to do without any human comfort." "And if I don't feel your comfort, let your will and your testing be my greatest comfort. For you won't stay angry forever, and you won't punish forever" (Psalm 103:9).

This chapter addresses one of our deepest human needs: the need for comfort. We all want relief from pain, reassurance in uncertainty, and peace in anxiety. The question is, where do we look for it?

À Kempis says we can't "find full comfort or complete joy in anything except God." Everything else—success, relationships, money, entertainment, even ministry achievements—offers only temporary, partial comfort. Only God provides the deep, lasting comfort our souls truly need.

We can trust that God is good, that He loves us, and that He's working all things together for our good (Romans 8:28). That doesn't mean everything that happens is good. It means God can use even bad things to accomplish His good purposes in our lives.

Wesley understood this deeply. His lifelong pursuit wasn't comfort in the worldly sense; it was what he called being "perfected in love," so rooted in God's love that even suffering couldn't shake his peace. That's the comfort à Kempis is after. Not the absence of pain but a soul so anchored in God that pain loses its power to destroy.

Try this: The next time pain shows up today, don't immediately reach for comfort. Sit with it and pray first.

Lord Jesus, be my comfort. Be my joy. Be my satisfaction. Teach me to look to you first when I'm hurting, not to distractions or temporary pleasures but to you. Help me be as ready to suffer as to rejoice, trusting that you are always working for my good. Protect me from seeking ultimate satisfaction in temporary things. When human comfort fails, and it will, remind me that you never fail. Be with me everywhere and always. Let me carry you wherever I go. And let this be my greatest comfort: nothing can separate me from your love. Amen.

47

All Our Cares Should Be Cast on God

Son, suffer me to do with thee what I please. I know what is expedient for thee. Thou thinkest like a man; thou judgest in many things, as human affection persuadeth.

—*The Christian's Pattern, 1741*

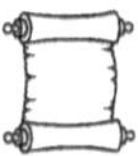

1. **Christ:** My child, let me do with you what I want. I know what's best for you. You think like a human. You judge many things based on your feelings.
2. **Christian:** Lord, you're right. You care for me more than I can care for myself. Anyone who doesn't give all their worries to you is on shaky ground (1 Peter 5:7). Lord, keep me committed to you. Then do with me whatever you want. Whatever you do with me can only be good.
3. If you want me to be in darkness, I bless you. And if you want me to be in light, I bless you. If you comfort me, I bless you. And if you allow suffering, I still bless you.
4. **Christian:** Lord, I'll willingly suffer whatever you allow to happen to me. I'll accept from you both good and bad, sweet and bitter, joyful and painful, and thank you for everything that happens to me. Keep me from sin, and I won't fear death or hell. As long as you don't reject me forever or erase me from the book of life (Revelation 3:5), whatever trouble comes won't really harm me.

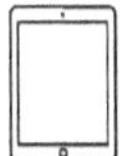

This chapter is about one of the hardest lessons in the Christian life: learning to let God be God. We want control. We want to decide what's best for us. We want to manage our own lives. But Christ says, "Let me do with you what I want. I know what's best for you."

I see this in parents with their children. Sometimes loving parents have to do things their kids don't want, like set boundaries, enforce consequences, or allow natural consequences to teach lessons. The child might protest, "You don't care about me!" But the opposite is true. The parents care so much that they're willing to let the child be upset in the short term for the sake of their long-term good. God's care for us is infinitely greater than the best parent's care for their child.

The response of the Christian in passage 3 is breathtaking in its completeness: "I'll accept from you both good and bad, sweet and bitter, joyful and painful, and thank you for everything." That's not resignation; that's faith. There's a world of difference between "I give up" and "I trust you." One is defeat; the other is surrender. And surrender, paradoxically, is where freedom lives.

Try this: Name one thing you're white knuckling right now. Say out loud, "I trust you," and loosen your grip.

Lord, I want to trust you completely with my life, but I confess I'm still holding the reins. I still flinch when the road gets dark. I still resist the bitter things, even knowing you use them for my good. Teach me to bless you in the darkness the same way I bless you in the light. Help me receive both the sweet and the bitter from your hand without panic or complaint. Give me faith to believe that your plan for me is better than my plan for myself, even when I can't see where you're taking me. Make me fully surrendered, not just in theory but in the daily practice of actually trusting you. Amen.

48

When People Wrong You and What True Patience Looks Like

What is it thou sayest, son? Cease to complain, considering my passion and that of my other saints. Thou hast not yet resisted unto blood.

—The Christian's Pattern, 1741

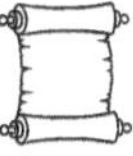

1. **Christ:** What are you saying, my child? Quit complaining. Think about my suffering and the suffering of my other saints. You haven't suffered to the point of death yet (Hebrews 12:4). Don't say, "I can't take this from someone like that," or "I shouldn't have to put up with this! He's wronged me terribly and accused me of things I never did." That's foolish thinking. It ignores what patience really means and who gets rewarded for it. Instead, it focuses on who hurt you and what they did.
2. You're not truly patient if you'll only put up with what you think is fair and only from people you like. But a truly patient person doesn't care who's testing them, whether it's someone above them, equal to them, or below them, whether it's a good and holy person or someone corrupt and unworthy. Instead, they accept all hardship equally, no matter how much, no matter how often, no matter from whom it comes, and they receive it all gratefully from God, seeing it as valuable. They know that nothing suffered for God, no matter how small, goes unrewarded.
3. So be ready to fight if you want to win. You can't win the crown of patience without a fight. If you refuse to suffer, you're refusing to be crowned. But if you want to be

crowned, fight bravely and endure patiently. There's no rest without effort. There's no victory without fighting.

4. **Christian:** Lord, make possible through your grace what seems impossible for me naturally. You know I can't endure much, and I get discouraged quickly when even small troubles come. Help me bear every trial willingly for your name. Suffering for you is good for my soul.
5. I admit my sin to you. I admit my weakness to you, Lord. Often just a small thing discourages and upsets me. I want to be brave, but when even a small temptation comes, it causes me great trouble. And when I think I'm somewhat safe and least expect it, I find myself knocked down by a small blow.
6. Look at how low I am, Lord, in my weakness; you know everything about me. Have mercy on me and pull me out of this mess so I don't get stuck and become completely defeated. O, mighty God of Israel, you who passionately love faithful souls, please see your servant's struggle and pain and help him in whatever he does. Give me heavenly strength, so that my old nature, this miserable flesh that still resists the Spirit, doesn't win.

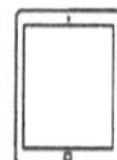

This is one of the most practical chapters in the entire book. It addresses something we all struggle with: how to actually be patient when people hurt us, mistreat us, or frustrate us.

À Kempis doesn't give us platitudes. He gives us reality. "You haven't suffered to the point of death yet." In other words, compared to what Jesus and the martyrs endured, our sufferings are relatively minor. That doesn't make them easy, but it does give us perspective.

I think about ministry. Some of my biggest frustrations don't come from major crises but from minor irritations, like the person who complains about the temperature in the sanctuary, the email full of criticism about something trivial, or the meeting that could have been an email. Small stuff. But it wears you down.

Wesley taught that Christian perfection meant being perfected in love, and love is patient (1 Corinthians 13:4). We grow in patience not by gritting our teeth but by letting God's love fill us so completely that it overflows even toward those who frustrate us. Real patience gets formed in exactly the situations we most want to escape.

Try this: Think of the person who's frustrating you most right now. Let God's love move through you toward them today.

God, the truth is I can't endure much. Small troubles knock me down, tiny frustrations get to me, and when someone criticizes me or misunderstands me, I fall apart faster than I'd like to admit. I want to be strong, but when the test actually comes, I discover I'm weaker than I thought. Don't let my old self, the impatient, easily offended, thin-skinned version, win. Change me into someone who can handle hard things without becoming bitter or resentful. Teach me to see suffering as a teacher, not an enemy. Give me the patience of your saints who endured so much more than I ever will. And remind me that you suffered first and that you are with me in it. Amen.

49

God Himself Is Better Than Anything He Gives

Above all things and in all things, O my soul, thou shalt ever rest in the Lord; for He is the everlasting rest of the saints.

—*The Christian's Pattern, 1741*

1. **Christian:** Above everything and in everything, my soul, you must always rest in the Lord, for He is the eternal rest of the saints. Let me rest in you, gracious and loving Jesus, above all created things, above all health and beauty, above all glory and honor, above all power and dignity, above all knowledge and wisdom, above all riches and skills, above all joy and happiness, above all hope and promise, above all merit and desire, and above all gifts and blessings you can give and pour out on us. Finally, let me rest in you above all the angels and archangels and all the armies of heaven, above all visible and invisible things, and above everything that is not you, my God.
2. For you, my Lord God, are best above all. You alone are most high, you alone are most powerful, you alone are completely sufficient, and you alone are sweet and full of comfort. And therefore, anything you give me besides yourself or reveal about yourself or promise me, as long as you yourself are not fully seen and possessed, it's all too little. For my heart cannot truly rest unless it rests in you, rising above all gifts and every created thing.
3. My beloved Jesus Christ, the purest lover, the ruler of all creation! If only I had wings of true freedom, that I might fly away and rest in you! When will I completely lose myself in you so that because of my love for you, I won't

even think about myself, but only you in a way that goes beyond all understanding, known only to those who've experienced it?

4. Jesus, brightness of eternal glory, comfort of the pilgrim soul! Come, O come! Without you, I have no joy. You are my joy, and without you, my life is empty. I'm miserable until you comfort me with the light of your presence and set me free.

5. Let others pursue whatever they want instead of you. But for me, nothing else brings joy except you alone, my God, my hope, my eternal salvation.
Christ: Look, I'm here! I've come to you because you called me. Your tears and the longing of your soul, your humility and the brokenness of your heart, these have brought me to you.

6. **Christian:** What more can your servant say except to greatly humble himself before you, always remembering his own unworthiness and sinfulness? For there is no one like you in all that is wonderful in heaven and earth. Your works are very good, your judgments true, and by your providence, all things are governed. Praise and glory be to you, O Wisdom of the Father! Let my mouth, my soul, and all creatures together praise and bless you.

This chapter is pure worship. It's a love song to God. And it addresses the deepest question of human existence: What will finally satisfy my soul?

I think about our cultural obsession with the next thing. The next purchase, the next vacation, the next achievement, the next relationship. We keep thinking, "If I just had this, then I'd be satisfied." But we get it, and the satisfaction fades, and we're on to wanting the next thing.

The only thing that truly satisfies is God Himself, not what He gives us but who He is.

Wesley experienced this deeply. His heart was "strangely warmed" at Aldersgate when he trusted in Christ alone for salvation. Not in his works, not in his religious activities, not in anything else, but in Christ alone. And that made all the difference.

Try this: Notice one moment today when something besides God is promising satisfaction. Don't bite. Come back.

Jesus, you're better than anything else I could have or achieve. Better than success, money, health, happiness, better than anything this world offers. I'm sorry for treating you like a vending machine, wanting your gifts more than you. Create in me a deeper hunger for you yourself. Help me stop chasing the next thing that promises satisfaction but never delivers. I want you, not just your blessings. Come close; without you, nothing else brings real joy. Thank you that you don't make me grovel; when I reach for you, you're already there. You're worth everything. Amen.

50

Remembering Everything God Has Done for You

Open, O Lord, my heart in thy law, and teach me to walk in thy commandments. Grant me to understand thy will and remember thy benefits, as well in general as in particular.

—*The Christian's Pattern, 1741*

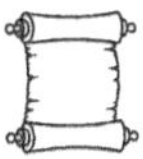

1. **Christian:** Open my heart to your ways, Lord, and teach me to follow your commands. Help me understand and remember all your blessings so I can thank you properly from now on. But I know I can't thank you enough for even the smallest of your gifts. I'm less than the least of all your blessings. And when I think about how generous you've been, the greatness of it overwhelms me.
2. Everything we have—inside and out, body and soul, natural and supernatural—all of it comes from you. You are generous, merciful, and good, and we've received every good thing from you. Though some people have received more and others less, it all belongs to you. Without you, we wouldn't have anything. Someone who has received more can't claim to be better than others. The person who's truly greater is the one who takes the least credit and is most humble and grateful.
3. Someone who has less shouldn't complain or envy those who have more. Instead, they should focus on you and praise your goodness because you give your gifts so generously, so freely, and so willingly without playing favorites. Everything comes from you, and therefore, you deserve praise in all

things. You know what's appropriate to give to each person and why one person has less while another has more.

4. Someone who truly loves you and recognizes your blessings should find their satisfaction in your will and your wise plan, not in comparing themselves to others. They should be so content and at peace that they'd be as willing to be the least as another person is to be the greatest. They'd be as content in last place as in first place, for your will and the desire to bring you glory should matter more than anything else.

This chapter is about changing our perspective from entitlement to gratitude. We live in a comparison culture. Social media feeds us an endless stream of other people's highlights, making us constantly aware of what we don't have. Someone always has more—more success, more money, more influence, more recognition.

À Kempis challenges this mindset. "Everything we have... all of it comes from you." Every breath, every talent, every opportunity, every relationship, it's all gift. We didn't earn it. We don't deserve it. It's grace.

The shift from comparison to contentment isn't passive; it's an act of faith. It's choosing to believe that God's distribution is wise even when it doesn't feel fair. As Paul learned in every circumstance, "I have learned, in whatever state I am, to be content" (Philippians 4:11). Learned, not received automatically. It's a discipline. And it starts with remembering what you already have.

Try this: Write down three things God has done for you that you haven't thanked Him for yet. Do it now.

God, help me see that everything I have is a gift from you. I confess I compare myself to others constantly, focusing on what I don't have instead of what I do. Shift my perspective from entitlement to gratitude. When I'm tempted to envy, remind me that you know what's best for me and why I have what I have. Make me genuinely content with your will, not just resigned but at peace. Let your will and your glory matter more than any blessing. Thank you for everything you've given me. Help me steward it faithfully. Amen.

51

Four Things That Bring Real Peace

Son, now will I teach thee the way of peace and true liberty.
Do, Son, that which another commandeth rather than thy own will.

—*The Christian's Pattern, 1741*

1. **Christ:** My child, now I'll teach you the way of peace and true freedom. Try to do what others want rather than what you want. Always choose to have less rather than more. Always seek the lowest place and to be beneath everyone else. Continually wish and pray that God's will would be completely fulfilled in you. Look, this kind of person enters into peace and quiet.
2. **Christian:** Lord, this short teaching has so much wisdom. You can do all things and always want what's best for my soul; give me more grace, so I can fulfill your instructions and work out my salvation (Philippians 2:12).
3. Lord, don't be far from me. Come close and help me because all kinds of harmful thoughts are attacking me, troubling my soul. How can I get through them without getting hurt? Do it, Lord, just as you say. Let all evil thoughts run from your presence. This is my hope, my only comfort, to run to you in every difficulty, to trust you, to call on you from my heart, and to wait patiently for your comfort.
4. Give me light, Lord Jesus, clear inner light. Drive all darkness from my heart. Stop my wandering thoughts. Break the power of temptations that violently attack me. Fight for me and defeat these evil forces, these seductive desires, so that peace can be established by your power, and your

praise can fill my pure heart. Command the winds and storms to stop. Say to the sea, "Be calm" (Matthew 8:26).

5. Send out your light and your truth to shine on me (Psalm 43:3). Pour out your grace from above. Let it refresh my heart like dew. Send streams of devotion to water my dry soul, so it can produce good fruit. Lift up my mind, weighed down by my sins. Draw all my desire toward heavenly things so that once I've tasted heavenly joy, earthly things won't interest me anymore.
6. Rescue me and free me from all the temporary comfort of created things. No created thing can fully comfort or satisfy my desire. Unite me to you with an unbreakable bond of love. You alone satisfy the person who loves you, and without you, everything else is pointless.

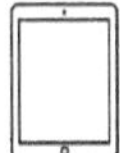

This chapter gives us a practical formula for finding peace. Not the fake peace that comes from having everything go our way, but the deep peace that remains steady even when life is chaotic.

Christ lays out four specific practices: try to do what others want rather than what you want, always choose to have less rather than more, always seek the lowest place, and continually wish and pray that God's will would be completely fulfilled in you. But notice what happens next. The Christian immediately says, "Lord, this is great wisdom... but I need your help to do it!" This is crucial. We can't manufacture this kind of peace through self-discipline. We need God's grace.

This is what real prayer looks like. Not polished and perfect, but raw and desperate. "I can't do this on my own. I need you."

Try this: Pick the one practice from this chapter that's hardest for you. Do just that one. Today.

Jesus, I want the peace you're describing, the deep peace that doesn't depend on my circumstances. But I need your help. I can't manufacture selflessness, simplicity, or surrender through willpower alone. Right now, my mind is full of anxious thoughts and darkness. Go before me; fight for me; open the prison doors. Calm the storms. Light up the dark places. Draw me toward you and give me a taste of your presence so satisfying that everything else loses its pull. You're the only one who truly satisfies. Amen.

52

Don't Get Distracted by Other People's Lives

Son, be not curious about the doings of others,
nor concern thyself with the affairs of thy betters.

—*The Christian's Pattern, 1741*

1. **Christ:** My child, don't be nosy. Don't stress about things that don't matter. What does this or that have to do with you? Follow me. Why do you care whether someone is like this or that? Whether they do or say this or that? You don't need to answer for others, only for yourself. I know everyone. I see everything that happens. I understand how things are with everyone, what they think, what they want, and what they're after. So, leave everything to me. But you, stay at peace and let people do what they're going to do. Whatever they do or say will come back on them because they can't fool me.
2. Don't chase after a great reputation or friendships with important people. Don't seek approval from certain people. These things distract you and fill your heart with darkness. I'd love to speak to you and share my secrets with you if you'd just watch for me and open your heart's door when I knock. Stay alert and pray. Stay humble in everything.

This chapter hits on something we struggle with constantly today: getting distracted by other people's lives. Social media has turned comparison and curiosity into an addiction. We scroll through feeds checking what others are doing, saying, and achieving. We compare their highlight reels to our behind-the-scenes. We wonder why they're more successful, more blessed, or more recognized than we are.

Christ's response is blunt. "What does this or that have to do with you? Follow me." In other words, stay in your lane. Focus on your own walk with God. You're not responsible for what others do; you're responsible for what you do.

The closing instruction is simple; "Stay alert and pray. Stay humble in everything." Don't get distracted. Keep your eyes on Jesus. Mind your own spiritual business.

Try this: Set your social media down for the rest of today. Use the time to ask God what He wants from you.

Jesus, I waste so much time being distracted by other people, comparing myself, worrying what they think, or keeping track of what they do. Help me stop. Remind me that I only have to answer for my own life. Teach me to mind my own business in the deepest sense—to focus on what you've called me to, not what you've called others to. Kill the comparison habit in me. Free me from the exhausting work of measuring myself against everyone around me. Keep me humble enough to know I'm not the standard; you are. Help me fix my eyes on you. Amen.

53

Where Real Peace Comes From

Son, I have said, Peace I leave with you, my peace I give unto you. I give not as the world giveth. All desire peace, but all care not for the things that truly belong to peace.

—The Christian's Pattern, 1741

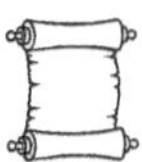

1. **Christ:** My child, I have said, "Peace I leave with you; my peace I give to you—not as the world gives do I give to you" (John 14:27). Everyone wants peace, but not everyone cares about the things that actually lead to peace. My peace is with those who are humble and patient. Your peace depends largely on endurance. If you listen to me and do what I say, you'll have a lot of peace.
   Christian: So, what should I do, Lord?
   Christ: Watch yourself in everything you do and say. Focus completely on this: pleasing only me and not looking for anything but me. Don't be quick to judge what others say and do. And don't get involved in things that aren't your business. Do this, and you'll rarely be troubled. But don't think you're special just because you're feeling spiritually good. Real spiritual maturity isn't found in those feelings.
2. **Christian:** Then where is it found, Lord?
   Christ: In giving yourself completely to God's will. Don't seek your own way, not in big things or small things, not now or ever. When comfort is taken from you, get ready for harder things. Don't make excuses as if you shouldn't have to suffer this much. Instead, admit that I'm right in whatever I allow, and praise my holy name. Then, you're on the true path of peace. And if you completely surrender yourself, you'll have peace in abundance.

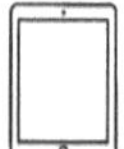

This chapter challenges our ideas about peace. We think peace means having everything go our way through comfortable circumstances, answered prayers, and smooth sailing. But Christ says real peace comes from something totally different: surrender.

"My peace is with those who are humble and patient." Not with those who have it easy. Not with those who get everything they want. But with those who learn to humbly accept whatever God allows.

That's the path to peace. Not the peace that depends on circumstances but the peace that remains steady no matter what happens. That is the peace Jesus promised, not as the world gives. In those rare moments when I've genuinely surrendered, when I've stopped fighting and started trusting, there's been this strange calm. Not because my circumstances changed but because I stopped needing them to.

Try this: Stop fighting one thing you can't control today. Say "I trust you" instead. Repeat as needed.

Jesus, I want your peace, the real peace, not the fake peace that depends on everything going my way. Teach me to be humble and patient, enduring hard things instead of constantly trying to escape them. Help me please you alone and stop worrying what others think or whether I'm getting what I want. Give me grace to surrender everything to your will. Help me stay grateful whether things are going well or falling apart. When comfort is taken away, help me trust that you know what you're doing. I want the deep peace that stays steady no matter what. Amen.

54

Prayer Is Better Than Reading

Lord, it is the work of a perfect man never to slacken his mind from the attentive thought of heavenly things and to pass without care among many cares.

—The Christian's Pattern, 1741

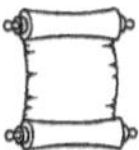

1. **Christian:** Lord, it takes a spiritually mature person to keep their mind on heavenly things and move through life's many concerns without being weighed down, not like someone who's checked out and doesn't care but with a free mind that isn't too attached to anything.
2. God, please protect me from getting tangled up in life's worries, from getting trapped by my body's needs, and from anything that could block my soul, so I don't get broken down by troubles and overwhelmed.
3. My God, you are sweetness beyond words. Make all earthly comfort taste bitter to me because it pulls me away from loving eternal things by offering me temporary pleasure. Don't let me be defeated, Lord. Don't let flesh and blood defeat me. Don't let the world and its short-lived glory deceive me. Don't let the devil and his tricks trip me up. Give me strength to resist, patience to endure, and consistency to keep going. Give me, instead of all worldly comforts, your Spirit's anointing. And instead of physical attraction and desire, pour love for your name into my soul.
4. Please guide me and teach me not to go to extremes.

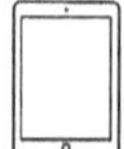

This chapter has a provocative title that might seem anti-intellectual: "Prayer Is Better Than Reading." But à Kempis isn't against learning. He's warning against using study as a substitute for actually connecting with God.

It's easy to read about God without actually talking to God. To study theology without practicing prayer. To consume Christian content, books, podcasts, sermons, without ever getting quiet enough to hear God's voice.

The closing request is wise: "Teach me not to go to extremes." We need balance. Not ascetic withdrawal from the world but healthy detachment. Not neglecting the body but not being ruled by it either.

For those of us in ministry who spend lots of time studying, this chapter is a needed reminder. All the Bible knowledge and theological training in the world won't substitute for actually praying.

Try this: Replace one session of reading or listening today with fifteen minutes of actual prayer. Just talking to God.

God, I confess I sometimes use reading and study as a substitute for actually spending time with you. Help me not substitute reading about you for actually talking to you. Don't let life's daily worries drown out your voice. Don't let my body's needs and desires rule me. Make me want you more than temporary pleasures. Protect me from the devil's tricks, the world's empty promises, and my own flesh's desire for the easy path. Give me strength to resist, patience to endure, and consistency to keep going. Guide me, teach me balance, and keep me from extremes. Amen.

55

Self-Love Gets in the Way

Son, thou oughtest to give all for all and to retain nothing of thyself. Know that the love of thyself doth hurt thee more than anything in the world.

—*The Christian's Pattern, 1741*

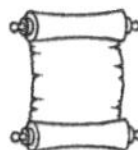

1. **Christ:** My child, you need to give up everything to have everything and keep nothing back for yourself. Understand this, self-love hurts you more than anything else in the world. Everything controls you more or less depending on how much you love it and cling to it. If your love is pure, nothing will enslave you. Don't want what you shouldn't have. Don't hang onto anything that might steal your inner freedom. It's strange that you won't give yourself completely to me from the bottom of your heart with everything you could want or have.
2. Why do you stress yourself with pointless grief? Why do you exhaust yourself with unnecessary worries? Follow my will and nothing will harm you. If you keep chasing this or that, wanting to be here or there to get your own way and enjoy yourself, you'll never be at peace or free from anxiety.
3. The solution isn't to get more stuff but to stop caring about it and to get rid of it completely from your heart. And I'm not just talking about money and possessions but also about chasing recognition and empty praise, all of which disappear with the world. Where you are won't help you much if you don't have the right attitude. You might change your circumstances, but you won't actually change yourself.

4. When a chance to change comes and you take it, you'll find not only what you were running from but a whole lot more. **Christian:** Strengthen me, God, through your Holy Spirit. Give me inner strength and help me let go of all this pointless worry. Give me heavenly wisdom, Lord, to learn to seek and find you above everything, to find my joy in you above everything, and to love you above everything.

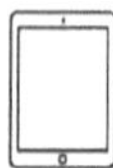

This chapter goes after the root issue that sabotages our spiritual lives: self-love. Christ's diagnosis is blunt; "Self-love hurts you more than anything else in the world."

The chapter describes the person who keeps "chasing this or that, wanting to be here or there" to find satisfaction. That's our culture in a nutshell, constantly searching for the next thing that will finally make us happy. But Christ says, "Something will always be missing in every situation, and everywhere you go, something will bother you."

The chapter includes an important warning: "You might change your circumstances, but you won't actually change yourself." How many times have we thought a new job, a new city, a new church, or a new relationship would solve our problems, only to discover we brought our same issues with us? External changes don't fix internal problems. The only thing that fixes self-love is replacing it with love for God.

Try this: Name one place where you keep rearranging your circumstances, hoping it will fix something internal. Stop. Pray.

vGod, I want to give myself to you completely, not just the easy parts, not just the parts I've already cleaned up, but everything. I know the thing I cling to most is the thing that controls me most, and I don't want anything controlling me except you. Show me what I'm still holding back. Give me the courage to let go of the comforts, the plans, and the self-protections I've been gripping so tightly. I don't want to be double-minded, promising surrender but then negotiating the terms. Help me actually do it, not just mean to do it. Make me the kind of person who gives you everything and trusts you with what comes next. Amen.

56

How to Call on God When You're Struggling

Blessed, O Lord, be thy name forever, who art pleased that this temptation and tribulation should come upon me. I cannot fly from it but must needs flee to thee.

—*The Christian's Pattern, 1741*

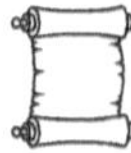

1. **Christian:** Lord, thank you, even though you've allowed this trouble to come to me. I can't escape it on my own. I need to run to you for help so you can turn this into something good for me. Lord, I'm struggling right now. I'm really troubled by what I'm going through. But maybe this is why I'm here, so you can be glorified when you lift me up from rock bottom. Lord, please save me. What can I do? Where can I go without you? Give me patience, Lord, right now. Help me, Lord, and I won't be afraid, no matter how bad this gets.
2. And now, in the middle of all this, what should I say? Lord, your will be done. I deserve this. I need to endure it. And I hope I can endure it patiently until the storm passes and things get better. But you can take this away from me or make it less intense, so it doesn't completely overwhelm me, just like you've done for me so many times before, my merciful God. And the harder this is for me, the easier it is for you because nothing is impossible for you.

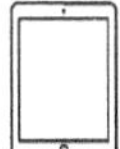

This chapter gives us a model for how to pray when we're really struggling. Not polished, perfect prayers, but raw, honest cries for help.

When we're overwhelmed, it helps to remember that our impossible situation isn't impossible for God. What crushes us is light work for Him. What seems like the end to us is just another opportunity for Him to show His power.

There's something in the Christian's response here worth sitting with. "I don't understand this, but I trust you." That's not weakness; that's the most mature prayer you can pray. It's the ability to stop demanding an explanation and start trusting the one who holds the outcome. À Kempis models a prayer that moves quickly from complaint to surrender, not because the pain isn't real but because he knows who he's talking to.

Try this: Stop asking "why" about your current struggle. Ask "what are you doing in this, Lord?" instead.

God, I'm struggling right now, and I can't fix this on my own, so I'm running to you, which is probably where I should have started. I need you to turn this into something good because on my own I can only see the mess. Forgive me for being so slow to bring my troubles to you. Forgive me for trying every other solution first. You are my helper and my deliverer, and I believe you can use even this for my good and your glory. So, I'm giving it to you—the fear, the confusion, the grief, all of it. Steady my heart. Show me what to do next. And help me trust that you've already seen the way through. Amen.

57

God Will Restore Your Strength

Son, I am the Lord that gives strength in the day of tribulation. Come unto me when it is not well with thee.

—*The Christian's Pattern, 1741*

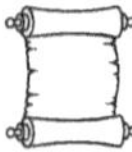

1. **Christ:** My child, I am the Lord who gives strength when you're going through hard times. Come to me when things aren't going well. Here's what blocks heavenly comfort: you're too slow to turn to prayer. Before you pray to me, you try everything else first, other comforts and external distractions. But now, catch your breath after the storm and get your strength back in my mercy. I'm here to fix everything, not just to restore it but to make it even better.

2. Is anything too hard for me? Am I someone who promises but doesn't deliver? Where is your faith? Stand firm and stay steady. Wait for me. Wait for me. I will come and heal you. Don't let your heart be troubled or afraid (John 14:27). Trust me and rely on my mercy. When you think you're farthest from me, I'm often nearest to you. When you think almost everything is lost, that's often when the greatest opportunity for growth is right there.

3. What I've given, I can take away, and I can give it back whenever I choose. When I give grace, it's mine to give. When I withdraw it, I'm not taking anything that's yours because every good and perfect gift comes from me (James

1:17). If I allow difficulty, don't complain or lose heart. I can quickly help you and turn all your pain into joy.

4. "As the Father has loved me, so I have loved you," I told my beloved disciples (John 15:9). And I didn't send them to temporary pleasures but to great struggles, not to honor but to being looked down on, not to laziness but to hard work, and not to rest but to produce fruit through patience. My child, remember this.

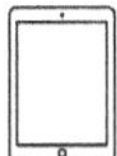

This chapter describes the rhythm of spiritual life that every believer experiences: strength, struggle, weakness, waiting, and restoration. Christ identifies the problem: "You're too slow to turn to prayer. Before you pray to me, you try everything else first, other comforts and external distractions."

We do this constantly. When we're stressed, we scroll our phones. When we're anxious, we binge entertainment. When we're hurting, we shop, eat, drink, or distract ourselves in a hundred different ways. We try everything except the one thing that would actually help: prayer. Prayer should be my first response, not my last resort.

But then comes the good news: "Catch your breath after the storm and get your strength back in my mercy. I'm here to fix everything, not just to restore it but to make it even better." God doesn't just patch us up. He restores us abundantly. He gives back more than we lost.

Try this: Identify the distraction you reach for first when life gets hard. The next time, reach for prayer instead.

God, comfort will come when the time is right. I believe that; help me believe it more. When you allow difficulty, keep me from complaining or losing heart because I know you can turn my pain into joy in an instant when it serves your purpose. Forgive me for looking for comfort everywhere except you. You are the one who gives strength in hard times, and I want to stop reaching for lesser things first. Help me breathe in the middle of the storm. Remind me that struggle and hardship are not signs of your absence but often signs of your work. And don't let me waste what you're teaching me right now. Amen.

58

Don't Let Anything Keep You from God

Lord, I stand in need of yet greater grace if I am to attain to that state wherein no man nor any creature may be a hindrance unto me.

—*The Christian's Pattern, 1741*

1. **Christian:** Lord, I need even more grace if I'm going to reach the place where no person or thing can keep me from you. As long as anything holds me back, I can't freely fly to you. What is more peaceful than having a single focus? And what is more free than someone who doesn't crave anything on earth? Unless you're free from attachment to created things, you can't freely focus on God. Anyone who thinks anything is great except God will stay small and stuck at ground level.
2. **Christ:** My child, you can't have perfect freedom unless you completely give up yourself. Everyone who loves themselves is trapped, full of desires, wandering aimlessly, and seeking self-indulgence instead of Jesus. Remember this short, perfect truth: Give up everything, and you'll find everything. Let go of craving, and you'll find rest.
Christian: Lord, that's not a one-day project. That short sentence contains all of spiritual perfection.
3. **Christ:** My child, don't give up or get discouraged when you hear about what spiritually mature people do. Instead, let it inspire you to reach higher, or at least make

you want it. I wish you'd reached the point where you were no longer focused on yourself but just stood ready to do whatever I ask.

4. And the purer someone's focus is, the more steadily they move through storms. It's rare to find someone who is completely free from self-seeking. So, your focus needs to be purified so it can be single-minded and aimed at me, beyond all the earthly distractions that get in the way.

This chapter is about the radical freedom that comes from not needing anything except God. À Kempis asks, "What is more peaceful than having a single focus? And what is more free than someone who doesn't crave anything on earth?"

We think freedom means having more options, more stuff, or more possibilities. But real freedom is actually the opposite; it's wanting so little that nothing can control you.

This sounds impossible. And the Christian's response is honest; "Lord, that's not a one-day project." No kidding. This is the work of a lifetime. But Christ doesn't say, "Too bad, figure it out." He says, "Don't give up or get discouraged. Let it inspire you to reach higher, or at least make you want it." That's the goal: pure, undivided focus on God. Not because we hate the world but because we've found something infinitely better.

Try this: Name one attachment that's keeping you at ground level. Hold it loosely today, just today.

Lord, I want to reach the place where I'm no longer focused on myself, where I'm not calculating what I get out of every situation but simply standing ready to do whatever you ask. I know I'm not there yet. There are still too many things I want, too many outcomes I'm trying to control, and too many conditions attached to my surrender. Loosen my grip on all of it. Make me free in the truest sense, free from the tyranny of my own desires and preferences. Teach me to hold everything lightly. Help me want what you want more than I want what I want. And grow me into someone whose one great ambition is simply to please you. Amen.

59

God Is Everything

My God and my all, what would I have more and what greater happiness can I desire?

—The Christian's Pattern, 1741

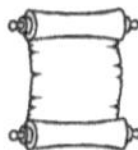

1. **Christian:** My God and my everything, what more could I want? What greater happiness could I ask for? What a beautiful and powerful phrase! But only for someone who loves you, not the world or the things in the world (1 John 2:15). "My God and my everything!" That says it all for anyone who gets it. When you're present, everything is delightful. But when you're absent, everything is awful. You give peace of heart, deep peace, and true contentment. You make us see everything in a positive light and praise you in everything. Nothing can satisfy us for long without you.
2. What wouldn't satisfy someone who experiences you? And what could possibly delight someone who doesn't delight in you?
3. O eternal light, surpassing all created lights, shine your brightness from above, reaching the deepest parts of my heart. Purify, fill with joy, enlighten, and bring life to my spirit, so I can cling to you with overwhelming joy. O, when will that amazing moment come when I'm filled with your presence and you're my everything? Until this happens, I won't have complete joy. My soul isn't at peace yet.
4. But you who rule the raging sea and calm its waves when they rise (Psalm 89:9), rise up and help me! There's no other hope or place to run except you, my Lord God.

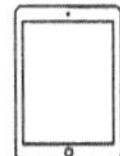

This chapter is a love song. It's the cry of someone who has discovered that God is the only thing that truly satisfies. "My God and my everything!" That phrase captures it all. Not "my God and a bunch of other good stuff," just "My God and my everything."

What makes this so powerful is the contrast: "When you're present, everything is delightful. But when you're absent, everything is awful." This isn't exaggeration. It's the honest experience of someone who's tasted God's presence. Once you've experienced God Himself, everything else loses its appeal.

I think about times when I've experienced God's presence in a real, tangible way. Everything else in my life looked different afterward. The things I was anxious about seemed smaller. The things I was chasing seemed less important. That's what this chapter is describing. The chapter asks, "What could possibly delight someone who doesn't delight in you?" Nothing. Nothing satisfies the human heart except God Himself.

Try this: Spend two minutes today saying nothing to God except "you are enough." Mean it as much as you can.

God, right now my soul is not at peace. I'm struggling and restless, still trying to find my rest in things that can't hold me. But you are my everything, and I know that somewhere in that simple truth is the peace I'm looking for. Help me stop chasing what can't satisfy and start resting in what can. Quiet the restlessness in me. When the world feels loud and demanding, draw me back to you. Teach me to say, "my God and my everything" and actually mean it, not as a phrase but as a lived reality. Be my portion. Be my peace. Be enough for me today. Amen.

60

Complete Surrender

Son, thou canst not possess perfect liberty, unless thou wholly renounce thyself.

—*The Christian's Pattern, 1741*

1. **Christist:** My child, let go of control, and you'll find me. Stop trying to control everything and claim things as yours. Give yourself up completely without taking it back.
   Christian: Lord, how often should I surrender myself? And how much should I let go?
   Christ: Always, every moment, in small things and big things. I make no exceptions. I need you to completely give up your own will. How else can you be mine and I be yours if you're not free from your own will, inside and out?
2. Some people surrender but not completely. They don't put their whole trust in God, so they're always trying to figure out how to take care of themselves. Some give everything at first, but when temptation hits, they take back what they gave up. These people don't grow spiritually. They'll never experience true freedom or the joy of being close to me unless they completely surrender, giving themselves to me daily.
3. I've told you this often, and now I'm saying it again: Let go of control. Give yourself up. And you'll find deep inner peace. Give everything for everything. Don't seek anything. Don't ask for anything back. Stay with me out of pure motives and complete trust in me, and you'll be free. Your heart will be free, and darkness won't have power over you. Let this be your prayer, let this be your desire, that you'd be

> completely free from all selfishness, that you'd follow Jesus with nothing of your own, and that by dying to yourself, you'd live forever with me.

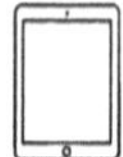

"Give everything for everything. Don't seek anything. Don't ask for anything back." This chapter is about the most radical form of freedom imaginable: having absolutely nothing to lose because you've already given it all away.

"Some people surrender but not completely." That hits close to home. We say, "I'm all in, God," but we keep a little reserve fund. We give God our lives, but we hold back our careers. We offer our time but not our weekends. We surrender our wills, but we keep veto power over anything too uncomfortable.

"Give everything for everything." That's the deal God offers. You give Him your small, finite, temporary everything, and you get His infinite, eternal everything in return. The question is, do we trust Him enough to make the trade?

Try this: Pick one thing you've been giving to God with strings attached. Cut the strings today.

Lord, I surrender control, not because it's easy but because you've made it clear I can't carry what I've been trying to carry. I keep taking things back after I've given them to you, and I'm tired of the cycle. Teach me what it actually looks like to let go, not just in the big dramatic moments but in the small daily choices where my will keeps asserting itself. I know complete surrender is the only path to real freedom, but I need your help to walk it. Every moment I try to hold on, remind me that I'm holding on to less than what you're offering me. Make me someone who trusts you enough to open my hands completely. Amen.

61

Mastering Yourself

Son, thou oughtest with all diligence to endeavor that in every place and action or external business, thou be inwardly free and master of thyself.

—The Christian's Pattern, 1741

1. **Christ:** My child, work hard to be internally free and in control of yourself in every situation. Make sure you control things, not the other way around. You should be in charge of your choices, not a slave to circumstances but a free person enjoying the freedom God's children have. Give temporary things minimal attention and keep your main focus on heavenly things. Don't let temporary things pull you in or control you. Instead, use them the way God intended.

2. If you stay steady in every situation and immediately bring everything to me in prayer, like Moses going to the tabernacle to ask God for guidance, you'll hear my answer and come back with direction about present and future things. Scripture tells us that Joshua and Israel were deceived by the Gibeonites because they didn't ask God first (Joshua 9:14). My child, always give your situation to me. I'll handle it well at the right time. Wait for me to work things out, and you'll find it turns out for your good.
   Christian: Lord, I gladly give everything to you because my own efforts accomplish so little.

3. **Christ:** My child, people often work hard to get what they want, but when they finally have it, they start wanting

something else. Human desires don't stay on one thing for long. So, it's actually a big deal to deny yourself, even in small things.

4. Real spiritual growth comes from denying yourself. But our enemy never stops tempting us. Day and night, he sets traps, hoping to catch people off guard. So, stay alert and pray, so you don't fall into temptation (Matthew 26:41).

"Work hard to be internally free and in control of yourself in every situation. Make sure you control things, not the other way around." This is one of the most challenging calls in all of Christian spirituality: be master, not slave.

We like to think we're in control of our lives, but the truth is most of us are controlled by something, including our schedules, our devices, our emotions, our appetites, other people's opinions, and our need for comfort.

The chapter gives a powerful image, "Like Moses going to the tabernacle to ask God for guidance." Before Moses made any decision, big or small, he went into the tent of meeting to seek God's guidance. What would it look like for us to do that? Not just praying about the big decisions but developing the habit of constant consultation with God. Before reacting to that text message. Before making that purchase. Before saying yes to another commitment. Before posting that comment.

Try this: Before your next decision today, go to God first, before you text anyone, Google anything, or decide.

God, I want to be free, genuinely free, not just free from obvious sin but free from being a slave to circumstances, to other people's opinions, or to my own moods and fears. I want to be the kind of person who gives temporary things temporary weight and eternal things eternal weight. Help me rise above the petty things that steal my peace. Teach me to hold lightly to comfort, reputation, and outcomes. Show me where I've let created things take up too much space in my heart. And fill that space with you, with the kind of eternal perspective that keeps me stable when everything around me is shifting. Amen.

62

No Glory Except in God

Lord, what is man that you are mindful of him? What has man deserved that you should give him your grace? Surely, I am nothing; I can do nothing; I have nothing that is good of myself.

—The Christian's Pattern, 1741

1. **Christian:** Lord, what is a human being that you care about him? Or the son of man that you think about him (Psalm 8:4)? What have humans done to deserve your grace? The truth is, Lord, I'm nothing. I can do nothing. I have nothing good in myself. In everything, I'm lacking, and I constantly drift back to nothing. Unless you help me and teach me from within, I become completely cold and fall apart.
2. But you, Lord, never change and last forever, always good, just, and holy, doing all things well, justly, and wisely. But I'm more likely to go backward than forward. I don't stay steady; I keep getting knocked down (Proverbs 24:16). Yet things quickly get better when you choose, and when you reach out to help me. You alone can help me without anyone else.
3. Thank you. You're the source of everything good whenever things go well with me. But I'm just nothing in your sight, an unsteady and weak person. So, what do I have to brag about? Why do I want people to think highly of me? For nothing! And that's the most pointless thing of all.
4. True glory and real joy come from celebrating you, not myself, from rejoicing in your name, not in my own achievements, and from finding joy in nothing except you. Let your name be praised, not mine. Let your work be

celebrated, not mine. In you, I'll celebrate and be joyful all day long. But as for myself, I won't boast except in my weakness (2 Corinthians 12:9).

5. Let people seek honor from one another. I'll only seek the honor that comes from God (John 5:44). All human glory, all temporary honor, all worldly success is nothing and foolishness compared to your eternal glory. O my truth, my mercy, my God, blessed Trinity, to you alone be praise, honor, power, and glory forever and ever.

"So, what do I have to brag about? Why do I want people to think highly of me? For nothing! And that's the most pointless thing of all." In an age of personal branding, platform building, and strategic self-promotion, this chapter feels like a bucket of cold water.

We're told to cultivate our image, manage our reputation, and highlight our achievements. LinkedIn profiles. Instagram highlights. Carefully curated public personas designed to make us look successful, influential, and important. And à Kempis is saying, "That's the most pointless thing of all."

When our identity is rooted in God rather than our performance, we're unshakeable. Criticism can't destroy us because we're not looking to people for our worth. Failure can't define us because we know our value comes from being God's children, not from our achievements.

"Let people seek honor from one another. I'll only seek the honor that comes from God." You can't seek God's approval and human applause at the same time. Only one of those pursuits leads to freedom.

Try this: The next time someone compliments you, give the credit away immediately to God, out loud or in your heart.

God, I confess I want credit for my work, my insights, my spiritual growth, and even my humility. Everything good in me is from you, every ability is a gift, and every opportunity is grace. Forgive me for taking credit for what you've done. Strip away my need to be recognized and praised. Teach me to celebrate your name, not build mine. When something good happens through me, help me be genuinely glad that you got the glory and not resentful that I didn't. I don't want a reputation; I want to be useful to you. You are my glory and the joy of my heart. I won't boast except in your mercy and my weakness. Amen.

63

Don't Put Your Peace in People

Son, if thou placest thy peace in anyone because he thinketh like thee and liveth with thee, thou shalt be unstable and entangled.

—The Christian's Pattern, 1741

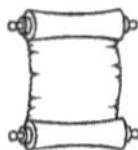

1. **Christ:** My child, if you base your peace on any person, because they agree with you or live near you, you'll be shaky and trapped. But if you turn to eternal truth, a friend leaving or dying won't destroy you. Your love for friends should be rooted in me. And for my sake, you should love anyone you care about in this life. No friendship lasts without me. No love is true and pure unless I'm holding it together. You should be so free from human attachments that you'd be willing to lose every human friendship if necessary.
2. Anyone who takes credit for good things blocks God's grace. The Holy Spirit's grace always looks for a humble heart. When you focus on created things, you lose sight of God. Learn to overcome yourself in everything because you love God, and then you'll know Him deeply. No matter how small something is, if you love it too much, it stains your soul and keeps you from enjoying God.

"If you base your peace on any person because they agree with you or live near you, you'll be shaky and trapped." Ouch. That lands hard. We do this constantly, don't we? We place our peace in people who validate us. We feel stable when people agree with us. We feel secure when we're surrounded by those who think like we do. And then someone leaves. Or disagrees. Or disappoints us. And our world falls apart.

À Kempis isn't saying friendship is bad. He's saying that when our peace depends on people rather than God, we're building on sand. "But if you turn to eternal truth, a friend leaving or dying won't destroy you." That's not cold; that's freedom. When your security is anchored in God, you can love people deeply without being controlled by them.

"No matter how small something is, if you love it too much, it stains your soul and keeps you from enjoying God." The path to freedom is loving people in God rather than instead of God.

Try this: Name one person whose approval you've been needing too much. Pray for them. Then release the need.

God, I confess I've placed my peace in people, needing their approval too much, being devastated when they disappoint me, and shaping my life around keeping them happy. And I'm tired of being that fragile. Teach me to ground my peace in you alone, the one thing that doesn't shift or change. Expose the small idols I've been loving excessively—the friendships, the validation, the need to be liked—and help me love people in you rather than instead of you. Kill my addiction to approval. Help me love people freely without needing them to sustain me. Root me so deeply in you that no human disappointment can knock me over. Amen.

64

Don't Chase Empty Knowledge

Son, let not the fair speeches and subtle sayings of men move thee: for the kingdom of God consisteth not in word, but in power.

—The Christian's Pattern, 1741

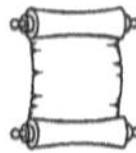

1. **Christ:** My child, don't let impressive speeches and clever arguments sway you. The kingdom of God doesn't consist of talk but of power (1 Corinthians 4:20). Pay attention to my words; they set the heart on fire and light up the mind. They convict you of sin and bring real comfort. Never read just to appear more learned or wise. Instead, work to destroy your sins; that will help you more than knowing answers to many difficult questions.
2. When you've read and learned many things, you must always come back to one thing. I'm the one who teaches people knowledge and gives children clearer understanding than any human teacher can. Whoever I speak to will quickly become wise and will grow a lot spiritually. But woe to those who chase after lots of interesting information from other people and don't pay much attention to serving me.
3. The time will come when the Master of masters will appear—Christ, the Lord of angels—to examine everyone's conscience. And then He'll search Jerusalem with a candle (Zephaniah 1:12). The hidden things of darkness will be exposed (1 Corinthians 4:5), and all human arguing will be silenced. I'm the one who teaches without noisy words or confusing opinions. I teach you to look down on

> earthly things, to dismiss what's temporary, to seek what lasts forever, to love eternal things, to avoid recognition, to endure wrongs, to place all your hope in me, to want nothing but me, and, above all, to love me with everything you have. I'm inside you, the teacher of truth, the one who searches your heart, who knows your thoughts, who leads you to do good.

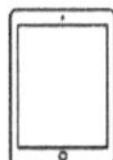

"Don't let impressive speeches and clever arguments sway you. The kingdom of God doesn't consist of talk but of power." This hits hard in our information-saturated world.

"Never read just to appear more learned or wise. Instead, work to destroy your sins; that will help you more than knowing answers to many difficult questions." That's a gut punch for those of us who love theology and who pride ourselves on being well read. He's not saying knowledge is bad. He's saying it's useless if it doesn't make us more holy.

Wesley put it plainly in a letter to the young preacher Joseph Benson (1768): "Beware you be not swallowed up in books! An ounce of love is worth a pound of knowledge." What does God actually want to teach us? Not theological systems but transformation. The Spirit's curriculum has no lectures, only a changed heart. Growth isn't measured by what we know. It's measured by how we love.

Try this: Measure your spiritual growth today by how you love, not by what you know.

God, forgive me for chasing knowledge instead of holiness, for reading books, consuming content, and collecting insights, while my actual obedience lags far behind my understanding. Strip away my intellectual pride. I don't need more information about you; I need more of you. Teach me from the inside, search my heart, discern my thoughts, and expose what's hidden. Stop me from chasing curious questions while neglecting simple obedience. Help me come back to one thing: loving you with everything I have. On the day you search my heart, may you find not impressive knowledge but genuine love, not clever arguments but actual transformation. Amen.

65

Trusting God When Criticized

Son, stand firm, and put thy trust in me. For what are words but words? They fly through the air but hurt not a stone.

—*The Christian's Pattern,* 1741

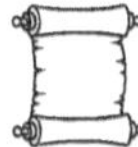

1. **Christ:** My child, stand firm and put your trust in me. What are words but mere words? They fly through the air but don't hurt a stone. If you're guilty, be willing to change. If you're innocent, be willing to suffer this for God's sake. It's a small thing to endure a few critical words if you don't yet have the courage to endure hard blows. Why do little things bother you so much? It's because you're still focused on the world and pay more attention to people than you should. You're afraid of being looked down on, so you don't want to be corrected for your faults. Instead, you look for excuses to hide behind.
2. But look closer at yourself, and you'll see that the world is still alive in you, along with an empty desire to please people. When you pull back from being humbled and criticized for your faults, it's clear you're not truly humble and not really dead to the world. But pay attention to my words, and you won't care about ten thousand words from others. Even if everything malicious that could be said against you were actually said, how could it hurt you if you completely let it go and thought of it as no more important than a speck of dust?
3. But whoever doesn't have inner strength and doesn't keep Jesus in focus is easily shaken by criticism. But whoever trusts in me and doesn't cling to their own judgment will be free from fearing people. For I'm the judge and the one

who knows all secrets. I know how everything happened. I know both the one who hurts and the one who suffers. I will judge both the guilty and the innocent. What people say often deceives. But my judgment is true; it stands firm and won't be changed.

4. A righteous person won't be troubled, no matter what happens to them from God (Proverbs 12:21). Even if a false accusation is made against them, they won't worry too much. For they know that I'm the one who searches hearts and minds (Revelation 2:23).
   Christian: Lord God, you're a just Judge, strong and patient. You know human weakness and sin; be my strength and what I completely trust in, for my own conscience isn't enough. Whenever I'm criticized, I should humble myself and accept it with grace. Your great mercy helps me more in getting forgiveness than any supposed righteousness I could claim in my defense because without your mercy, no one alive will be justified in your sight (Psalm 143:2).

"What are words but words? They fly through the air but don't hurt a stone." If only we actually believed that. How much emotional energy do we waste on what other people say about us?

The chapter offers incredible freedom. "Stand firm and put your trust in me." Not "defend yourself." Not "make sure everyone understands your side." Just stand firm. Trust God. Let the words fly. The response to criticism is actually simple: If it's true, own it and change. If it's false, endure it and trust God.

Words only have the power we give them. If our identity is anchored in God, criticism becomes background noise. Painful, maybe. Annoying, certainly. But not destructive. God knows the whole story. He knows the context. He knows your heart. He knows their heart. He knows what's true and what's not. And His opinion is the only one that ultimately matters. We don't need to prove we're right. We need mercy.

Try this: The next time criticism lands, ask two questions: Is it true? If so, change. If not, let it go.

God, I give you my reputation, the thing I've been guarding and defending and worrying about far too much. I confess I care too much about what people say, spend too much energy defending myself, and lose too much sleep over criticism. Teach me to ask two honest questions when I'm criticized: Is this true? If so, help me change. Is this false? If so, then help me endure it quietly. Kill my need to make sure everyone understands my side. You are the only judge who matters, and you already know the whole story. Forgive me for caring more about human approval than your glory. Be my defense, my strength, and the only verdict I need. Amen.

66

Longing for Eternity

O blessed mansion of the heavenly city! O most clear day of eternity, which night obscureth not, but the highest truth ever enlighteneth!

—The Christian's Pattern, 1741

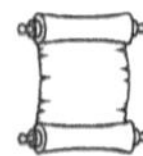

1. **Christian:** Heaven, that incredible place where God lives! Eternity, a day that never ends, never gets dark, where God's truth is the only light we need! A day of constant joy and complete peace that never changes or fades. I wish that day would finally come, and all these temporary things would be over! The saints in heaven see it clearly, shining with endless brightness. But those of us still on earth? We only see it from far away, like looking through a cloudy mirror. Jesus, when will I finally stand before you? When will I see the glory of your kingdom? When will I be with you in your kingdom, the place you've been preparing for the people you love since before time began?
2. Comfort me during my exile. Ease my sorrow, for I want only you. My God, don't be far from me. Draw all my attention to you. Make me forget all the things of this world. Help me immediately reject sinful thoughts. Come, heavenly joy, and let all impurity run from me. Pardon me, too, and mercifully forgive me whenever I think about anything besides you during prayer. I honestly confess that I'm constantly distracted. Often, I'm not really present where I physically am. I'm somewhere else, wherever my thoughts carry me. Where my thoughts are, there I am.
3. But blessed is the person who, for you, Lord, lets go of all created things, fights hard against their sinful desires, and

> through spiritual passion, puts to death the lusts of the flesh so that with a clear conscience they can offer pure prayer to you and be worthy to join the angels with all earthly things shut out, both outwardly and inwardly.

"Heaven, that incredible place where God lives! Eternity, a day that never ends, never gets dark, where God's truth is the only light we need!" There's an ache in the human heart that nothing on earth can satisfy.

C.S. Lewis described it perfectly, "If I find in myself a desire which no experience in this world can satisfy, the most probable explanation is that I was made for another world."[1]

I saw this ache made real in my grandfather. The last time I was with him, my twin boys were toddlers. He sat up in bed, weak but still clear as a bell, and talked about heaven. Not abstract theology. He spoke about it like he was describing a place he was about to visit. And then he turned to me and said, "Won't it be wonderful?" In that moment, longing for heaven became real to me. My grandfather wasn't afraid. He was anticipating. He was ready to go home.

The chapter also acknowledges a very practical problem: distraction. "I honestly confess that I'm constantly distracted." How many times have we sat in worship, knelt in prayer, or opened our Bible, but our minds were somewhere else entirely?

Try this: Catch yourself being mentally absent from God today. When it happens, come back. That's the whole practice.

---

1. Lewis, C.S. Mere Christianity. Touchstone: New York, 1996.

God, my heart aches for home, for the day when all tears are wiped away, all separation ends, and I see you face to face. I'm tired of the exile, tired of the struggle, and tired of how easily I get distracted from what I'm really longing for. Comfort me in the meantime. Don't let the enemy's schemes—the distractions, the temptations, the lies—make me forget what I'm actually waiting for. Forgive me for being mentally absent while physically present; my body shows up, but my mind wanders. Draw all my attention to you. Sustain me until the day I'm finally home. You're what I'm longing for. Come quickly, Lord Jesus. Amen.

67

Fight Valiantly for Heaven

Son, when you perceive the desire of everlasting bliss to be given you from above, open your heart wide, and receive this holy inspiration with your whole soul.

—The Christian's Pattern, 1741

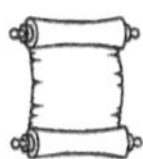

1. **Christ:** My child, when you feel the desire for eternal joy given to you from above, open your heart wide and receive this holy gift with everything you have. Give heartfelt thanks to heaven's goodness that treats you so well, comes to you so mercifully, and holds you up strongly so you don't sink back to earthly things through your own weakness. You don't get this desire by thinking it up or working for it but only as a gift of heavenly grace.
2. My child, often the fire is burning, but the flame doesn't rise without smoke. In the same way, some people's desires burn toward heavenly things, yet they're not free from fleshly temptations. For what's mixed with self-interest isn't pure and perfect.
3. Don't ask for what's pleasant and profitable to you but for what pleases me and honors me. You'd like to be in the glorious freedom of God's children right now (Romans 8:21), but that time hasn't come yet. There's still another season, a time of war, a time of hard work and testing. I am the highest good. Wait for me patiently until God's kingdom comes.
4. You still need to be tested on earth and trained in many things. Comfort will sometimes be given but not the full abundance of it yet. Be strong. Be brave both in doing and in suffering things that go against your nature. You must

put on your new nature (Ephesians 4:24) and be changed into a different person. You must often do what you don't want to do and give up what you do want to do.

5. Others will have great reputations; nothing will be said about you. Others will be given responsibilities; you'll be considered useless. It's a great thing if you bear it quietly. There's hardly anything where you need to die to yourself more than in seeing and suffering things that go against your will.
6. Consider, my child, the result of these struggles, how quickly they end and how great the reward is. There, I'll give glory for the insults you suffered here, joy for sorrow and, for the lowest place, a seat in my kingdom forever (Luke 14:10). There, the fruit of obedience will show, the hard work of repentance will bring joy, and humble submission will be gloriously rewarded.
7. Now, therefore, bow humbly before everyone. Don't find joy in this or that, only in being humbled and in pleasing me and bringing me honor alone. Whether through your life or through your death, may God always be glorified in you (Philippians 1:20).

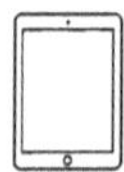

Have you ever had one of those moments, in worship, in prayer, or in Scripture, where something opens up inside you and you feel the pull of heaven? A longing that this world simply can't satisfy? That desire isn't something you worked up; it's a gift from above. Treat it like one.

À Kempis says, when that happens, receive it. Open your heart wide. Give thanks. Don't analyze it to death. But then the warning: check your motives. "What's mixed with self-interest isn't pure and perfect." Even our spiritual desires can be tangled up with what we want for ourselves.

"What pleases others will succeed; what pleases you won't." If you've been in ministry any length of time, you know this feeling.

Dying to self isn't giving up chocolate for Lent. It's submitting when you disagree and continuing when you see no results. Eugene Peterson called it, "a long obedience in the same direction." That's the whole chapter. And the whole Christian life.

Try this: Name one place you've been serving for recognition. Keep doing it, but offer it to God alone today.

Lord, thank you for those moments when I feel the pull of heaven. Teach me to receive those gifts with open hands and not try to recreate them on my own terms. Purify my desires. I confess that even my prayers for spiritual things get tangled up with what I want for myself. Strip away the self-interest. Help me want what you want more than what I want. Forgive me for resenting the process. When I'm overlooked, remind me that you see. When I'm dismissed, remind me that you hear. Keep me faithful in the meantime. Bow my will to yours. And let the end make it all worth it. Amen.

68

When You Feel Abandoned by God

Lord God, Holy Father, be thou blessed both now and for evermore because as thou wilt, so is it done, and what thou dost is good.

—The Christian's Pattern, 1741

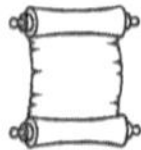

1. **Christian:** Lord God, holy Father, blessed are you, now and forever. Whatever you want is what happens, and whatever you do is good. Let me find joy in you, not in myself or anything else. You alone are the true source of joy. You're my hope and my crown. You're my joy and my honor, Lord. What do I have that I didn't receive from you without deserving any of it? Everything is yours. Sometimes my soul is so sorrowful I could cry. Sometimes it's troubled within me because of the difficulties hanging over me.

2. I long for peaceful joy. If you give peace, if you pour holy joy into my heart, then I'll be full of gladness and devoted to praising you. But if you pull away, I won't be able to follow your commands. Instead, I'll humble myself because it's not like it was before when your light shone on me and I was protected under the shadow of your wings from the fierce temptations that attacked me.

3. O righteous Father, forever worthy of praise, the time has come when I'm being tested. Beloved Father, it's fitting that I should suffer something for you now. The time has come when for a little while I would be beaten down outwardly but inwardly I would live forever with you.

4. It's grace for your friend to suffer and be afflicted in the world for love of you, no matter how often it happens. Nothing happens on earth without your approval and

purpose or without a reason. It's good for me, Lord, that you've afflicted me so I can learn your righteous ways and remove all pride and arrogance from my heart.

5. There's no one under heaven who can comfort me except you, my Lord God, the heavenly Healer of souls, who wounds and heals, who brings down to the grave and raises up again (1 Samuel 2:6). Discipline me and let your correction teach me.
6. Look, heavenly Father, I'm in your hands. I humble myself under your discipline. Discipline me however you need to so my stubborn heart is shaped by your will. Make me your holy and humble follower, ready to respond to your gentlest leading.
7. Help me, Lord, know what should be known, love what should be loved, praise what pleases you most, value what's precious to you, and reject what's worthless in your eyes. Don't let me judge by what I see or form opinions based on what uninformed people say. Instead, help me discern spiritual things with true judgment and above all things, always seek your will and what pleases you.

This chapter describes what spiritual writers call "the dark night of the soul" when God feels absent, prayer feels empty, and faith feels like pushing against a wall. You're doing everything right—praying, reading Scripture, serving faithfully—but God feels a million miles away. And nobody talks about this enough. We celebrate mountaintop experiences and answered prayers, but we don't prepare people for the valleys.

À Kempis is clear: This season is part of the plan. God knew it was coming. He allowed it. And He has a purpose in it, to scrub away pride, to redirect us from seeking comfort in people and circumstances, and to teach us to rely on Him alone rather than on feelings of His presence.

The chapter uses a powerful image: "you, my Lord God, the heavenly Healer of souls, who wounds and heals, who brings down to the grave and raises up again." That's not cruelty; that's surgery. The wound is purposeful. The darkness isn't abandonment; it's formation.

C.S. Lewis said, "Relying on God has to begin all over again every day as if nothing had yet been done."[2] The dark night strips away everything we've been relying on besides God Himself. And that, painful as it is, is exactly the point.

Try this: If God feels distant right now, don't run. Stay. Keep showing up. That's not failure; that's faithfulness.

God, I feel like you've abandoned me, but I know you haven't, so I'm choosing to trust that over what I feel. Prayer feels empty, Scripture feels dry, and faith feels like work right now. But this chapter reminds me, you knew this season was coming. It's not punishment; it's preparation. So, I'm humbling myself under your discipline and trusting you're teaching me not to rely on feelings or consolation but on you alone. Strip away whatever my stubborn heart needs stripped away. You wound to heal and bring down to raise up. Help me trust the process. Don't let me waste this season. And when you bring me through, let me emerge more dependent on you than I was before. Amen.

2. Lewis, C.S. Letters to Malcolm: Chiefly on Prayer. HarperOne, 2017.

69

You Don't Deserve Comfort (But God Gives It Anyway)

Lord, I am not worthy of thy comfort, nor of any spiritual visitation, and therefore, thou dealest justly with me when thou leavest me poor and desolate.

—*The Christian's Pattern, 1741*

1. **Christian:** Lord, I'm not worthy of your comfort or any spiritual blessing. You're being fair to me when you leave me poor and empty. Even if I could cry an ocean of tears, I still wouldn't be worthy of your comfort. The truth is, I deserve nothing but punishment and discipline because I've seriously offended you and sinned greatly in many ways. But you, O merciful God, don't want anyone to die. To show how incredibly good you are, you comfort me in ways no human ever could.
2. What have I done, Lord, that you should give me any heavenly comfort? I can't remember doing anything good. I've always been quick to sin and slow to change. What do I deserve except hell and eternal fire? I honestly confess I deserve nothing but contempt and rejection.
3. What can I say, guilty and ashamed as I am? I have nothing to say except this: I have sinned, Lord, I have sinned. Have mercy on me. Pardon me. What do you want most from a guilty, miserable sinner? That they be broken hearted and humble themselves for their sins. From true brokenness and a humble heart comes hope of forgiveness. A guilty conscience is reconciled to God. God's favor, once lost, is

restored. And God and the repentant soul meet together with a holy kiss (Psalm 85:10).

4. A broken and humble heart over sin is an acceptable sacrifice to you, Lord. It's far sweeter to you than incense smoke (Psalm 51:17). For you never turn away a broken heart (Psalm 51:17).

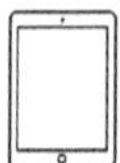

"Lord, I'm not worthy of your comfort or any spiritual blessing." This chapter captures one of the great paradoxes of the Christian faith: The more we understand grace, the more we realize we don't deserve it. But that's not discouragement; that's progress. Only when we see ourselves clearly can we truly appreciate grace.

The chapter is brutally honest. "I can't remember doing anything good. I've always been quick to sin and slow to change." There's a difference between low self-esteem and accurate self-assessment. Low self-esteem says, "I'm worthless and God can't use me." Accurate self-assessment says, "I'm a sinner saved by grace, and any good in me comes from God."

God doesn't require perfection before we come to Him, just honesty and humility. "From true brokenness and a humble heart comes hope of forgiveness. A guilty conscience is reconciled to God. God's favor, once lost, is restored. And God and the repentant soul meet together with a holy kiss." When we stop defending ourselves and humbly admit our sin, God doesn't reject us; He embraces us. God never turns away a broken heart.

Try this: Come to God today with nothing to offer but your need. No performance. Just honesty.

Lord, I'm not worthy of your comfort; I can barely remember doing anything good that wasn't tangled up with selfish motives. I've been quick to sin and slow to repent, and I have nothing to offer except a broken heart and an honest confession. But here I am, anyway, coming not because I've earned it but because of your grace. I believe you don't turn away a broken and honest heart; that's who you are. So, I come poor and empty, asking you to fill what I can't fill myself. Forgive me. Heal me. Restore what sin has disfigured. I have nothing to bring but my need. And apparently, that's enough for you. Amen.

70

Sinful Nature vs. Grace

Son, mark diligently the motions of nature and grace, for they move in a very contrary and subtle manner.

—The Christian's Pattern, 1741

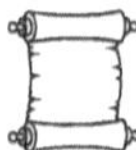

1. **Christ:** My child, pay close attention to the movements of sinful nature and grace because they work in very subtle ways and can only be understood by someone who is spiritually aware. Everyone claims to want good things in their words and actions. That's why many people are fooled by appearances of goodness. Sinful nature is sneaky, seductive, and entangling. It deceives many and always works for its own benefit. But grace walks in honesty, does everything purely for God, uses no deceit, and finally rests in God alone.
2. Sinful nature refuses to die willingly, refuses to be held down, refuses to be defeated, and refuses to submit. But grace practices self-denial, resists sensual desires, welcomes discipline, is willing to submit, and chooses not to demand her own freedom. Sinful nature fights for her own advantage. But grace doesn't focus on what benefits herself but rather what helps many others. Sinful nature eagerly accepts honor and respect. But grace faithfully gives all honor and glory to God.
3. Sinful nature fears shame and being looked down on. But grace is happy to suffer insults for Jesus' name. Sinful nature loves comfort and physical rest. But grace can't sit idle and gladly takes on hard work. Sinful nature focuses on temporary things, celebrates earthly gain, grieves over loss, and gets angry at every little insult. But grace thinks

about what lasts forever, doesn't cling to temporary things, and isn't upset by harsh words because she has placed her treasure and joy in heaven.

4. Sinful nature is greedy and prefers to receive rather than give. But grace is generous to everyone, avoids self-interest, is content with little, and believes it's more blessed to give than to receive. Sinful nature is drawn to created things and wandering around. But grace draws people to God and to goodness, lets go of created things, runs from the world, and hates fleshly desires.
5. Sinful nature does everything for her own gain and profit. She does nothing for free but hopes to get something equal or better in return. But grace seeks nothing temporary, requires no reward except God alone.
6. Sinful nature is happy to have many friends and relatives, fawns over the powerful, and flatters the rich. But grace loves even her enemies and isn't impressed by having many friends. She favors the poor over the rich and feels more for the innocent than the powerful.
7. Sinful nature refers everything to herself, fighting and arguing for herself. But grace brings everything back to God, from whom it all originally came. She doesn't argue or put her opinion before others, but in every understanding and opinion, she submits herself to God's eternal wisdom and divine judgment. She doesn't want herself or her things to be praised but wants God to be praised in His gifts, who out of pure love gives everything.

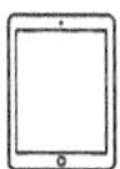

"Pay close attention to the movements of sinful nature and grace because they work in very subtle ways." This chapter describes the civil war that rages inside every Christian, the battle between our sinful nature and God's grace.

Sinful nature asks, "What's in it for me?" Grace asks, "How can I serve?" Sinful nature craves recognition; grace gives all glory to

God. Sinful nature demands comfort; grace is willing to sacrifice. The scary part is that sinful nature is sneaky. It whispers reasonable sounding things, like that we need to take care of ourselves first and that we have a right to defend our reputation. All true in some sense, but all easily hijacked by self-interest.

So how do we choose grace over sinful nature? Wesley would say, through the means of grace—prayer, Scripture, fellowship, communion, and fasting. But we also have to be ruthlessly honest with ourselves about our motives. When grace is truly operating, we're genuinely glad for God to be praised while we stay in the background. That's what transformation looks like. That's grace winning.

Try this: Name one place sinful nature is winning this week. Ask God for grace to let grace win instead.

God, I feel the war inside me. Sinful nature is sneaky, disguising selfishness as wisdom and making comfort sound like virtue. Expose my mixed motives. Reveal when I'm serving myself while pretending to serve you. Let your grace be stronger than my sinful nature. Teach me to die to myself daily. Help me choose what's right when it costs me something, love when it would be easier to defend myself, and serve without calculating the return. Not for my glory. For yours. Through Jesus Christ your Son, amen.

71

We Need Grace to Overcome Our Sinful Nature

Lord my God, who hast created me after thine image and likeness, grant me this grace which thou hast shewed to be so great and so necessary for salvation.

—The Christian's Pattern, 1741

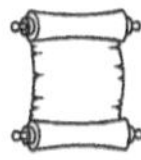

1. **Christian:** God, you created me in your image. Give me the grace I desperately need to overcome my sinful nature that keeps dragging me toward sin and destruction. I feel it constantly; there's a law of sin at work in my body that fights against what my mind knows is right. It holds me captive in so many ways (Romans 7:23). I can't resist it unless your grace, poured powerfully into my heart, helps me.
2. Lord, I desperately need your grace to start any good work, to keep going, and to finish it. Without it, I can do nothing. But with you, I can do all things when your grace strengthens me (Philippians 4:13). O heavenly grace! Without you, even our best actions are nothing, and no natural gifts matter at all. Talent, wealth, beauty, strength, intelligence, eloquence, none of it means anything to you, Lord, without your grace.
3. What an amazing gift grace is! It makes the spiritually poor become rich in virtues, and it makes those who are blessed with much stay humble in heart. Come to me now. Fill me with your comfort before I collapse from exhaustion and spiritual dryness. Your grace is enough for

me, even when I don't have other things my sinful nature wants (2 Corinthians 12:9).

4. Your grace is the source of truth, the teacher of discipline, the light in my heart, my comfort when I'm hurting; it is what drives away sorrow, what casts out fear, what nourishes devotion. It is the spring of repentant tears. What am I without grace? Nothing but a dry stick, worthless and ready to be thrown away. So please, Lord, let your grace go before me and follow me. Make me always eager to do good works through Jesus Christ your Son. Amen.

"Without it, I can do nothing. But with you, I can do all things when your grace strengthens me." This chapter is about total dependence on God. That's a hard pill to swallow in a culture that glorifies self-made success, bootstrapping, and personal achievement. But it's biblical truth. Jesus said it plainly, "Apart from me you can do nothing" (John 15:5).

"Lord, I desperately need your grace to start any good work, to keep going, and to finish it." From start to finish, it's all grace. "Talent, wealth, beauty, strength, intelligence, eloquence, none of it means anything to you, Lord, without your grace." All our natural gifts are worthless without grace. You can't think your way into holiness. You can't buy your way into righteousness. You need grace.

Without it, we are "nothing but a dry stick, worthless and ready to be thrown away." But if you have grace, you have everything you need.

Try this: Ask God for grace today, not just to finish well but to begin. Right now. This is the beginning.

God, I need your grace. I can't overcome my sinful nature on my own. I've tried. I keep doing what I don't want to do and failing to do what I should. Pour your grace into my heart; I need it to start, to continue, and to finish. All my natural gifts are worthless without you. Only grace can save me, transform me, and make me holy. Come down to me. Fill me before I collapse from dryness. Your grace is sufficient, even when everything else is lacking. Let it go before me, follow me, and work in me, making me diligent in good works through Jesus Christ your Son. Amen.

72

Deny Yourself and Follow Jesus

Son, he that endeavoreth to withdraw himself from obedience withdraws himself from grace.

—The Christian's Pattern, 1741

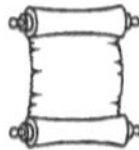

1. **Christ:** Follow me. I am the way, the truth, and the life. Without the way, there is no going. Without the truth, there is no knowing. Without the life, there is no living. I am the way you should follow, the truth you should trust, and the life you should hope for. I am the only way, the highest truth, the true life, yes, the blessed life, the eternal life. If you stay on my path, you will know the truth, and the truth will set you free, and you will take hold of everlasting life.
2. If you want to enter life, keep the commandments. If you want to know the truth, believe me. If you want to be my disciple, deny yourself. If you want to be lifted up in heaven, humble yourself on earth. If you want to reign with me, carry the cross with me. For only those who take up the cross find the way of joy and true light.
3. **Christian:** Lord Jesus, since your life was humble and rejected by the world, give me grace to follow you in facing the world's rejection. For the servant is not greater than his master, nor the disciple above his teacher. Train me in your life, for in it my salvation and true holiness are found.
4. **Christ:** My child, now that you know these things, you'll be blessed if you do them. Anyone who has my commandments and keeps them, that's the one who loves me. And

I will love them, and I will reveal myself to them and seat them with me in my Father's kingdom.
Christian: Lord Jesus, as you've said and promised, let it happen. I have received the cross. I have received it from your hand. I will carry it and carry it until death, as you have laid it upon me. Truly the life of a Christian is the cross, but the cross is a guide to paradise.

5. So, let's take courage, brothers and sisters, and go forward together. Jesus will be with us. For Jesus' sake, we've taken up this cross, and for Jesus' sake, let's keep going with the cross. He will be our helper, the one who is our guide and goes before us. Look, our King goes before us, and He will fight for us.

"Follow me. I am the way, the truth, and the life." This is Jesus' invitation. But it's not an invitation to comfort; it's an invitation to the cross.

We like the first part of Jesus' invitation, "Follow me." We love the idea of being close to Jesus, walking with Him, learning from Him. But we often miss what following Jesus actually means, picking up a cross. The chapter lays out the non-negotiable conditions of discipleship: If you want truth, believe Him; if you want to be His disciple, deny yourself; if you want to be lifted up, humble yourself; and if you want to reign with Him, carry the cross with Him. Every one of those comes with a cost.

"For only those who take up the cross find the way of joy and true light." The cross isn't an obstacle on the way to paradise. It is the way. The Puritan preacher William Gurnall put his finger on why we so often fail to pick it up: "We fear men so much because we fear God so little." We're not bearing our crosses alone; we're a community going forward together.

Try this: Name the cross you've been avoiding. Pick it up today. You're not carrying it alone.

Jesus, you are the way, the truth, and the life. I want to follow you, but I want to follow without the cross. I want glory without suffering, and the crown without the crucifixion. But you're clear: deny yourself, take up the cross, and follow. Give me grace to do that. Help me renounce myself; kill my need for recognition, comfort, and approval. Make me willing to be misunderstood, overlooked, and rejected, as you were. I've taken up the cross. I can't turn back. Let's go forward together. Jesus will be with us. Amen.

73

Don't Be Crushed by Your Weakness

Son, patience and humility in adversity are more pleasing to me than much comfort and devotion in prosperity.

—The Christian's Pattern, 1741

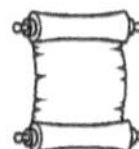

1. **Christ:** My child, patience and humility in hard times please me more than great comfort and devotion when things are going well. Why are you upset over every little criticism? Even if it had been much worse, you shouldn't have been shaken. But now let it go. It's not anything new . It's not the first time this has happened, and it won't be the last if you live long enough. You're brave enough when things are going well. You can give good advice and encourage others with your words. But when trouble suddenly comes to your door, you're left with no wisdom or strength, so see how weak you really are. Nevertheless, it's meant for your good when these and similar things happen to you.
2. I am still here, says the Lord, ready to help you and to give you greater comfort than before if you put your trust in me and call earnestly on me. Learn to be more patient and prepare yourself for greater suffering. It's not over if you often feel troubled or badly tempted. I am the one who will strengthen and heal those who are hurting and lift up to heavenly glory those who know their own weakness.
3. **Christian:** Lord, blessed are your words, sweeter to me than honey and the honeycomb. What would I do in so

many troubles and difficulties unless you comforted me with your holy words? What does it matter how much or what I suffer, as long as I reach the safe harbor of salvation in the end? Give me a good ending. Give me a safe journey out of this world! Remember me, my God, and guide me on the right path to your kingdom. Amen.

"You're brave enough when things are going well. You can give good advice and encourage others with your words. But when trouble suddenly comes to your door, you're left with no wisdom or strength." This chapter is uncomfortably accurate.

We're all strong until we're not. We can handle criticism until it hits too close to home. We can endure hardship until it lasts longer than we expected. "So, see how weak you really are." How many times have we been knocked down by something small? A critical comment. An unexpected setback. And we're surprised every time.

"Patience and humility in hard times please me more than great comfort and devotion when things are going well." It's easy to be spiritual when everything's going well. The real test is what happens when things fall apart. "I am still here, says the Lord, ready to help you." Feeling weak doesn't mean you're failing. It means you're human. "What does it matter how much or what I suffer, as long as I reach the safe harbor of salvation in the end?" We don't need a perfect journey. We just need to finish well.

Try this: Let the next small thing that knocks you down today teach you something instead of defeat you.

God, I'm strong until I'm not, and right now, I'm not. I fall apart over small things, get knocked down by criticism, and feel crushed by setbacks that shouldn't shake me this much. I give good advice to others but can't follow it myself. Forgive me for being spiritually confident in the good times and falling apart when trouble actually arrives. Help me learn patience, real patience, not just gritting my teeth but trusting that you are doing something in this. Strengthen me when I'm weak. Heal me when I'm hurting. Remind me that it's not over when I feel troubled because you're still here, ready to give me more comfort than before. And help me finish well. Amen.

74

Don't Try to Figure Out God's Secret Plans

Son, beware thou dispute not of high matters, nor of the secret judgments of God.

—The Christian's Pattern, 1741

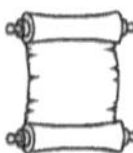

1. **Christ:** My child, don't argue about deep mysteries or try to understand God's secret judgments. Why is this person left behind while that person is lifted up? Why is this person so troubled while that person is so greatly blessed? These things are beyond human understanding. No amount of reasoning or debate can figure out God's judgments. So, when the enemy plants these questions in your mind, answer like the prophet, "You are just, Lord, and your judgments are right." And again, "The judgments of the Lord are true and righteous altogether" (Psalm 19:9). God's judgments are to be respected and honored, not argued about or analyzed.
2. Don't argue or debate about which saints are holier than others or which ones are greater in the kingdom of heaven. These debates often create conflict and pointless arguments. They also feed pride and empty glory, which then produce envy and division. I am the one who made all the saints. I gave them grace. I will give them glory. I know what everyone deserves. I knew them before the world was made. I chose them out of the world. I called them by grace. I drew them by mercy. I led them safely through various temptations. I poured glorious comforts

into them. I gave them perseverance. I will crown their patience.

3. I know both the first and the last. I embrace them all with endless love. I am to be praised because of all my saints. I am to be blessed above all things and to be honored in every single one of them.

"Why is this person left behind while that person is lifted up? Why is this person so troubled while that person is so greatly blessed?" But the chapter says, stop. These things are beyond human understanding. "No amount of reasoning or debate can figure out God's judgments." God's ways are not our ways. His thoughts are not our thoughts (Isaiah 55:8–9).

The right response isn't "I understand your judgments" but "I trust your character," not "I can explain your ways" but "You are just, Lord, and your judgments are right."

God's response to Job's demands for explanation was simply, "Where were you when I laid the earth's foundation?" (Job 38:4). And Job's answer? "I spoke of things I did not understand, things too wonderful for me to know" (Job 42:3). "I am to be praised because of all my saints. I am to be blessed above all things." Just trust that He's just, He's good, and He knows what He's doing.

Try this: Stop demanding an explanation for one thing you don't understand about God. Trust His character instead.

God, I confess I want to understand your secret plans—why you bless some and not others, why some prayers get answered and others don't, why some people suffer so much, and others seem to sail through life. But that kind of understanding isn't mine to have, and my craving for it is really just another form of wanting to be in control. Forgive me for arguing with your ways instead of trusting your character. You are just. You are good. You see the whole story, and I only see a page. Teach me to rest in that. Help me stop demanding explanations and start trusting the God who doesn't owe me any. You know what you're doing. That's enough. Amen.

75

Put All Your Hope in God Alone

Lord, what is my trust in this life? Or what is my greatest comfort of all the things under heaven? Is it not thee, my Lord God, whose mercies are without number?

—*The Christian's Pattern, 1741*

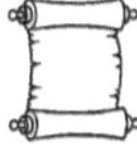

1. **Christian:** Lord, what do I trust in this life? What gives me the most comfort of all things under heaven? Is it not you, my Lord God, whose mercies are countless? When have things ever gone well for me without you? Or when could things be bad when you're with me? I'd rather be poor with you than rich without you. I'd rather be a wanderer on earth with you than possess heaven without you. Where you are, there is heaven. And where you're not, there is death and hell. I have no one else to trust and no one who can help me when I'm in need, except you alone, my God. You are my hope. You are my confidence. You are my comfort, and most faithful to me in everything.
2. Everyone looks out for themselves. You alone pursue my salvation and turn everything to my good. Even when you allow me to face temptations and hardships, you arrange all of this for my good. You test those you love in countless ways. In these trials, you deserve just as much love and praise as when you fill me with heavenly comfort.
3. In you, Lord God, I put all my hope and find my refuge. I rest on you in all my troubles and distress. Friends can't help. Powerful allies can't assist. Wise counselors can't give useful advice. Books can't bring comfort. Wealth can't save.

No hidden or peaceful place can protect me if you don't help, strengthen, comfort, teach, and keep me safe.

4. For all things that seem to bring peace and happiness are nothing without you. You are the ultimate good, the fullness of life, and the source of all wisdom. To you, I lift up my eyes. In your great goodness and abundant mercy, look on me and hear the prayer of your humble servant. Protect my soul amid the many dangers of this fallen world and guide me on the path of peace to the land of eternal light.

"Where you are, there is heaven. And where you're not, there is death and hell." Everything leads to this: God is everything, and without God, we have nothing.

"I'd rather be poor with you than rich without you." That's radical. Most of us would say, I'd rather have God AND be rich. But à Kempis goes further: "I'd rather be a wanderer on earth with you than possess heaven without you." Even heaven is worthless without God.

The chapter strips away every substitute one by one; "Friends can't help. Powerful allies can't assist. Wise counselors can't give useful advice. Books can't bring comfort. Wealth can't save." Only God can do what only God can do.

But here's the turn that makes this more than resignation: "Even when you allow me to face temptations and hardships, you arrange all of this for my good." Not just "God is all I have" but "God is all I need, even when it doesn't feel like it." Do you have God? Or are you using God to get other things? Because at the end of the day, God alone is enough.

Try this: Name one thing you've been using God to get. Surrender it. Then see if God Himself turns out to be enough.

Lord, I want both, you and wealth, comfort, and success. Forgive me for looking everywhere but you for help and for trusting in people, money, and my own cleverness when none of those can save me. You are my hope, my confidence, and my comfort, the only truly reliable thing in my life. Everything outside of you is temporary and ultimately disappointing. So, I put all my hope in you. Be my dwelling place. Be my peace. Be enough. Amen.

THE CHRISTIAN'S PATTERN — BOOK FOUR

HOLY COMMUNION

PREFACE

Recovering Wesley's Vision of Holy Communion

If you're a modern Methodist, you're about to read something that might surprise you. Book Four of *The Imitation of Christ* is entirely about Holy Communion, and John Wesley loved it so much he translated the whole book. The surprise is Wesley's high view of the sacraments. Most contemporary Methodists celebrate communion monthly, quarterly, or even less frequently. We think of it as a memorial, a symbolic remembrance of what Jesus did. But Wesley believed it was more. Much more.

Wesley's Unchanging Conviction

John Wesley first published *The Christian's Pattern* in 1735, before his famous Aldersgate experience on May 24, 1738. Wesley's theology of Holy Communion remained remarkably consistent throughout his entire life. The proof? Look at his sermon "The Duty of Constant Communion" (Sermon #101), which he published in 1787, more than fifty years after he first translated à Kempis. In that sermon, Wesley argues passionately that Christians should take communion as often as possible. He doesn't say monthly. He doesn't say quarterly. He says as often as you can. Wesley believed communion was a "means of grace," one of the primary ways God meets with His people, forgives sins, strengthens faith, and transforms lives.

The 166 Hymns

In 1745, John and Charles Wesley published *Hymns on the Lord's Supper*, a collection of 166 hymns about communion. These hymns are theologically rich, biblically grounded, and experientially powerful. They express real presence (Christ truly meets us in the sacrament), sacrificial memorial (we remember and proclaim Christ's death), means of grace (God strengthens, sanctifies, and transforms us through communion), pledge of glory (the sacrament points forward to the heavenly feast), and covenant renewal (we recommit ourselves to Christ at the table). The Wesleys didn't write 166 hymns about something they considered optional or unimportant.

What Wesley Believed (and Didn't Believe)

Wesley did believe that Christ is truly present in communion through the Holy Spirit, that the sacrament is a powerful means of grace, that God strengthens and transforms us through communion, and that Christians should receive communion frequently. Wesley's view can be described as a "real spiritual presence." In other words, Christ is truly present but spiritually rather than physically. This is a middle path between Catholic transubstantiation and bare memorialism. Book Four of *The Christian's Pattern* is the richest, most devotional section of the entire work. Read it slowly. Let it draw you into deeper communion with Christ. And then, go to the table.

Why This Matters for Modern Methodists

Here's the challenge: Most modern Methodists have lost Wesley's vision of Holy Communion. We've reduced it to a symbol. A nice reminder. A monthly obligation. We've settled for crumbs when Wesley offered us a feast. This is a tragedy, not just historically (we've lost our heritage) but spiritually (we've lost a powerful means of grace).

Imagine if you received communion every Sunday, or even more often, expecting to encounter Christ there, expecting to be strengthened and transformed, expecting grace to flow into your life. Imagine approaching the table not with boredom or routine but with hunger, expectation, and joy.

That's Wesley's vision. That's what Book Four invites you into.

What to Expect in Book Four

Fair warning, Book Four of *The Imitation of Christ* is intense. Thomas à Kempis wrote from a medieval Catholic context, and some of his language reflects that. He talks about priests consecrating the elements, he uses bridal imagery about union with Christ, and he expresses passionate devotion that might feel foreign to modern evangelicals. But don't let that scare you off. Yes, we'll need to filter some things through our Protestant convictions. Yes, some language will need cultural translation.

But the heart of Book Four is profoundly biblical and deeply Wesleyan: Come to the table hungry. Expect to meet Christ there. Confess your sins beforehand. Surrender yourself completely. Receive grace gratefully. Leave transformed.

These 15 chapters will challenge you to take communion more seriously, prepare your heart more carefully, receive the sacrament more frequently, expect more from the table, and experience deeper union with Christ.

How to Use This Book

Here's my recommendation:

Before communion Sunday: Read one or two chapters from Book Four. Reflect on the questions raised. Pray the prayers provided. Examine your heart.

Come to the table expectantly.

After communion: Read Chapter 84 on offering yourself to God in response to what you've received. Reflect on what you experienced. Thank God for meeting you there. Ask for grace to live differently this week.

In your small group: Discuss Wesley's vision of constant communion. Share honestly about your experiences at the table. Pray for each other's spiritual hunger to increase. Challenge your church to offer communion more frequently.

Wesley's vision of constant communion isn't just historical trivia; it's a spiritual invitation. Book Four is your guide into that vision. Come to these chapters hungry.

A Personal Word

Last summer, I walked the Peak Wesley Way in England with my friend and mentor, Pastor Jorge Acevedo. For five days, we hiked through the Derbyshire hills, following the paths John Wesley and his preachers once traveled.

Every morning before we set out, we celebrated Holy Communion together. It transformed the pilgrimage.

Starting each day at the table—receiving Christ, remembering His sacrifice, and being filled with His presence—gave us strength for the journey ahead. We weren't just walking Wesley's paths; we were practicing Wesley's piety.

Here's the question: How often do you want to commune with God? Once a month? Once a quarter? Or every day? The word "communion" itself gives us the answer. If you want to commune with your Maker, why would you voluntarily skip opportunities to do so?

Wesley understood this. He celebrated communion every Sunday and took it whenever it was offered. He wrote 166 hymns about it. He preached about "constant communion" even at age 84.

He knew something we've forgotten: The table is where Jesus promised to meet us.

Don't miss the meal.

One Final Note

You might be thinking: "But my church only offers communion once a month (or quarter). What am I supposed to do?"

Here's what you can do: Attend every time communion is offered. Don't skip. Make it a priority. Prepare carefully. Read Book Four. Examine your heart. Come hungry. Receive expectantly. Believe that Christ will meet you there. Trust that grace will flow. Talk to your pastor. Share Wesley's vision. Ask about offering communion more frequently. Visit other churches when yours doesn't celebrate. Start praying. Ask God to restore a hunger for the sacrament in Methodist churches across the land.

Wesley's vision of constant communion isn't just historical trivia. It's a call to return to our roots. And Book Four is your guide. Now turn the page and let Thomas à Kempis, through John Wesley's eyes, teach you to love the Lord's table again.

Come hungry.

Come expectant.

Come ready to meet Jesus.

76

Approaching Communion with Reverence

Come to me, all you who are weary and burdened,
and I will give you rest.

—*The Christian's Pattern, 1741*

The Voice of the Disciple:

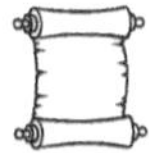

1. These are your words, Christ, the eternal truth. Because they're yours, I receive them with gratitude and faith. You spoke them for my salvation. These words, full of grace and love, draw me in. But my own sin makes me hesitate.
2. You tell me to come boldly, to receive the food of eternal life, to share in your life. "Come to me," you say, "all you who are weary and burdened, and I will give you rest" (Matthew 11:28). And I have to stop and ask, Who am I that you would say that to me? The highest heaven can't contain you, and you're inviting me to the table?
3. How can I come when I see nothing good in myself? How can I bring you into my house when I've offended you so many times with my careless living? Angels and archangels stand in awe of you. Saints and righteous people tremble before you. And you say, "Come to me"? Nobody would believe it if you hadn't said it yourself.
4. Noah was a righteous man, and he spent a hundred years building the ark just to be saved with a handful of people. How can I prepare myself in an hour to receive the Maker of the world? Moses built a sacred chest from imperishable

wood just to hold the stone tablets. Solomon spent seven years building a temple just to honor your name. And I? How can I bring you into my house? How carelessly I come to your table.

5. And yet, what Noah's ark held was a shadow. What Moses built was a symbol. What Solomon constructed pointed forward. You are what all of it was pointing to. David danced before the ark with everything he had. How much more should I come to your table with my whole heart, burning with gratitude and awe?
6. God, Creator of everything that exists, what you do in this sacrament is breathtaking. Hidden grace flows here. Spiritual strength is given. Lost strength comes back. Beauty that sin disfigured is restored. Sometimes this grace is so real that even the body feels it.
7. It's heartbreaking that our coldness keeps us from running to this table. Christ is offered here, the one in whom all hope rests. And he's offered not in one place but everywhere so that His grace and love might reach as many people as possible. Thank you, Jesus, Good Shepherd, for feeding us weary travelers with your own body and blood and for calling us with your own voice, "Come to me, all you who are weary and burdened, and I will give you rest."

"How can I bring you into my house, when I've so often offended you with my careless living?" This chapter asks a question most modern Christians never ask: Are we taking communion too casually? For many of us, communion has become routine. But this chapter says, Wait. Do you understand what's happening here?

The chapter uses three Old Testament examples—Noah's ark, Moses' tabernacle, and Solomon's temple—to show how seriously people used to take meeting God. The question is devastating; "How can I in one hour prepare myself to receive the Maker of the world?" Come to the table. But come with reverence. Come with joy. Because the Lord of heaven is offering Himself to you.

Try this: Before your next communion, spend five minutes in actual preparation. Examine your heart. Arrive ready.

Jesus, I confess I've taken communion casually. I've treated it as routine, something to get through on my way to lunch. I haven't prepared my heart. I haven't come with reverence. Help me approach your table with the reverence it deserves. I'm not worthy. I see nothing good in myself. I've offended you with my careless living. But you've graciously invited me, not because I deserve it but because you love me. In this sacrament, give me spiritual grace. Restore the strength I've lost. Return the beauty that sin has disfigured. Refresh me, poor wanderer that I am, with your precious body and blood. Help me never take this mystery for granted. Amen.

77

God's Love Displayed in Communion

Trusting in your goodness and incredible mercy, I come to you, Lord.

—The Christian's Pattern, 1741

The Voice of the Disciple:

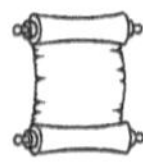

1. Trusting in your goodness and incredible mercy, I come to you, Lord. I come sick, needing a healer. I come hungry and thirsty, desperate for what only you can give. I come with empty hands to the one who is the source of everything. You know me. You see that I have nothing in me that deserves this. So, I simply confess how unworthy I am and acknowledge how good you are. Thank you; you're doing this not because I've earned it, but so that your goodness might be known, your love made visible, and your grace put on display.
2. Jesus, merciful, holy, and kind, how much gratitude and reverence you deserve from me just for letting me come to your table. Nothing is better than this: bowing completely before you and praising you for your endless goodness. I will lift you up. I will stand in the truth of my unworthiness, not in despair but in wonder that you would have me at all.
3. You are the Holy of Holies. I am a sinner. You bend down to me, though I'm not worthy to look up at you. You come to me. You want to be with me. You invite me to your feast.

You want to give yourself to me as living bread, the bread that came down from heaven and gives life to the world.

4. Stop and think about what's actually happening here. The God who spoke and created everything, who commanded and it was done, is giving Himself to us as food. This is love without limit. Grace without explanation. Power and tenderness in the same moment. Thank you doesn't come close. But thank you. Thank you. Thank you.
5. Keep my heart and body clean so I can come to your table again and again with a clear conscience, celebrating this mystery and this gift you established for your honor and as a living memorial to what you've done.
6. Let my soul rejoice and give thanks for such an extraordinary gift in the middle of this hard world. Every time I receive the body of Christ, I'm participating in my own redemption and sharing in everything Christ won. His love never diminishes. The greatness of His sacrifice never runs out. So come to this table with fresh eyes every time. Let it feel as significant as if Christ were being born this very day, or as if He were hanging on the cross right now, suffering and dying for you.

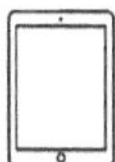

"Why would you come to me? Who am I that you should give yourself to me?" This is the question that should blow our minds every time we take communion. We can grasp God creating the world. We can grasp God sending prophets. But God giving us Himself at the table? That's incomprehensible.

"How can a sinner like me stand before you?" This is the scandal of communion. In the Old Testament, sinners could not approach God's presence directly. But now, Jesus invites sinners to the table. Not the righteous. Not those who have it all together. Sinners. Broken people. Us.

"You're doing this for your own sake, not because I've earned it, but so that your goodness may become more widely known." It's not about our worthiness. It's about His grace. Every communion is Christmas. Every communion is Good Friday. Every communion is Easter. And the only answer to "Why would God do this?" is love. Extravagant, incomprehensible, sacrificial love.

Try this: The next time you take communion, receive it as if it's the first time. Let the strangeness of it land.

Jesus, I'm asking the same question this chapter asks: Why would you come to me? Who am I that you should give yourself to me? I'm a sinner. I'm unworthy. And yet here you are, inviting me to your table. Thank you for doing this, not because I deserve it but so your goodness and love might be revealed. I come hungry and thirsty, desperate for what only you can give. Help me never take this for granted. Every time I come, help me see it with fresh wonder. Your love never diminishes. The greatness of your sacrifice is never exhausted. Feed me. Strengthen me. Transform me. Amen.

78

The Benefits of Frequent Communion

I will not send them away hungry, or they may collapse on the way.

—The Christian's Pattern, 1741

The Voice of the Disciple:

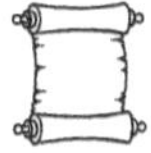

1. Lord, I come to you to be fed and to delight in this holy feast you've prepared for people like me. You are everything I could need or want. You are my salvation and my redemption, my hope and my strength. Make my soul glad today; I'm lifting it up to you. I want to receive you now with real devotion. I want to bring you into my life like Zacchaeus, desperate for a glimpse of you and transformed when you showed up at his door. My soul is thirsty for you. My heart longs to be close to you.
2. Give me yourself and that's enough. Nothing else satisfies. I can't go on without you; without your presence in my life, I'll give out along the way. This is exactly what you promised when you said you wouldn't send people away hungry. Don't send me away hungry. You left yourself in this sacrament for people like me, weary travelers who can't make it on their own. You are the nourishment my soul needs. Whoever receives you will share in everlasting life.
3. What kind of love is this? You, the Creator of everything, the source of all life, come to a hungry soul and fill it

with yourself completely. Think about what it means to receive Christ at the table. You're receiving the Lord of the universe as your closest friend. You're welcoming the one who knows everything about you and loves you anyway. You're embracing the one whose love surpasses every other love, whose beauty outshines everything beautiful, whose wisdom has no end. Let heaven and earth go quiet for a moment. Nothing compares to this.

"I must often come to you and receive you for my soul's well-being, or I'll collapse along the way." This chapter makes the case for frequent communion simple: We need it. We need it the way we need food.

Jesus said He wouldn't send people away hungry. The chapter says, deal with me in the same way, you who left yourself in the sacrament for the comfort of the faithful. He left Himself in the sacrament so we wouldn't faint along the way.

We often treat communion as optional. But à Kempis is saying, you need this. Your soul can't survive without it. The Zacchaeus reference is perfect; he was desperate to encounter Jesus, and his whole life was transformed when Jesus came to his house. We can invite Jesus in through communion and be changed. So come to the table. Often. Regularly. Hungry for what only Christ can give.

Try this: If your church offers communion this week, go. If it doesn't, find one that does. Don't faint along the way.

Jesus, I need you. I don't just want you; I can't make it without your presence. So, I'm coming to your table, not out of routine but out of genuine need. You are my salvation and my strength, my hope and my redemption. Everything I need is found in you. Give me yourself and that's enough. I must often come to you, or I'll collapse along the way. You said you wouldn't send people away hungry. Don't send me away hungry. My soul thirsts to receive you. Like Zacchaeus, I'm inviting you in. Come in. Bless me. Change me. Feed me with yourself. Amen.

79

The Gifts Given to Those Who Receive Communion Devoutly

My Lord God, come to your servant with the blessings of your sweetness.

—The Christian's Pattern, 1741

The Voice of the Disciple:

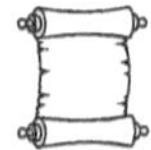

1. Lord God, come to me with the gift of your sweetness so I can approach your table the way it deserves. Stir up my heart. Break through this heavy numbness I carry. Meet me with your salvation so I can taste what's hidden in this sacrament. Open my eyes to see what's really happening here and strengthen my faith to believe it without needing to feel it first. This is your doing, not mine. Your institution, not a human invention.
2. Lord, with a simple and honest heart, trusting your word and taking you at your promise, I come to you. I believe you are truly present here in your body and blood. I ask for your mercy and your grace so that I can be filled with love for you and stop looking everywhere else for what only you can give. This sacrament is the health of my soul and body, the remedy for everything that's broken in me. Through it, old patterns are broken, temptations lose their grip, grace pours in, faith grows stronger, hope gets confirmed, and love catches fire.
3. You give so much to those who come to you here, Lord, my God, the one who guards my soul. You lift them out of discouragement and into hope. You refresh and renew them so that the person who came to the table anxious

and numb leaves feeling the difference. That's not routine. That's transformation.

4. You do all this so that we learn the truth about ourselves, that we have nothing on our own and everything through you. Left to ourselves, we're cold, hard, and flat. Through you, we come alive. Who comes humbly to a flowing spring and leaves with nothing? Who stands close to a fire and feels no warmth? You are a spring that never runs dry, a fire that never goes out.
5. So even if I can't drink from the fullness of that spring, I'll put my mouth to it and take what I can. Even if I can't burn like an angel, I'll get close enough to feel the warmth. Whatever I'm missing, Lord, you who invite everyone who's weary and burdened to come and find rest, make up the difference.
6. I'm worn out. Grieved. Loaded down with failures. Troubled by temptation. Tangled up in things I can't seem to escape. There's no one else who can help me. Just you, my Lord, my Savior. I give you everything. Keep me. Lead me home. Receive me for the glory of your name, you who prepared your body and blood to be my food and drink.

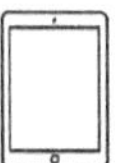

What does communion actually do for us? À Kempis gives a remarkable list: vices are healed, passions restrained, temptations lessened, grace poured in, faith strengthened, hope confirmed, and love kindled. That's not a memorial. That's a means of grace.

"You are a fountain always full and overflowing, a fire ever burning and never going out." Even if we can't experience the fullness of God's grace every time, we can put our mouths to the fountain. Something will happen. Some warmth will reach us. Come weary, burdened, and troubled. He's waiting. He'll receive you and make you better.

Try this: Come to the table this week with one specific need. Expect something. See what God does.

Jesus, I confess I haven't expected much from communion. I've treated it like a ritual, something to get through. But you say this sacrament is the health of soul and body, the remedy for all spiritual sickness. I want to believe that. Help my unbelief. Stir up my heart. Free me from this heavy spiritual numbness. Help me come with expectation and real faith that you are here, and you are good. Because I'm coming to you, weary, burdened, tormented, and troubled. There's no one else who can help me but you alone. Receive me. Feed me. Transform me. Amen.

80

The Dignity of the Sacrament and the Role of Ministers

If you had the purity of an angel and the holiness of John the Baptist, you still would not be worthy to receive or administer this sacrament.

—The Christian's Pattern, 1741

The Voice of Christ:

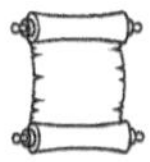

1. Even if you had the purity of an angel and the holiness of John the Baptist, you still wouldn't be worthy to receive or lead this sacrament. No human effort earns the right to handle what's happening here, to celebrate communion and receive the bread of heaven. This is a profound mystery. What's given to those who minister at the table isn't even given to angels. The ordained minister in the church is the one authorized to consecrate and serve the body of Christ, acting as God's servant, using God's word by God's command. But God Himself is the real author and the invisible worker behind it all.
2. Trust what God says about this sacrament more than what you can see or feel. Approach this with respect and holy awe. If you've been called to lead at the table, you haven't been given an easy job. You've been held to a higher standard and called to deeper holiness. A minister should be marked by genuine virtue and give others a model worth following, not with a life like everyone else's but with a life oriented toward heaven.
3. A minister clothed in sacred vestments takes Christ's place, humbly praying to God for the people and for the ministry

> itself. Before and behind is the sign of the Lord's cross, a constant reminder of the passion of Christ. The cross worn on the front is a call to follow in Christ's footsteps and study to imitate them. The cross worn behind is a call to endure quietly and gently whatever hardship others bring. The cross in front calls for mourning over personal sin; the cross behind calls for compassionately carrying the weight of others' sin. And when a minister celebrates at the table, God is honored, the angels rejoice, the Church is strengthened, the living are helped, rest is given to the dead, and the minister becomes a partner in every good thing.

This chapter is about the weight of what happens at the table. "You should believe God Almighty in this most excellent sacrament more than your own sense or any visible sign." Faith over feeling. We may not sense anything when we take communion. But Christ is present, not because we feel Him but because He promised.

Those who lead communion carry a particular responsibility: "You must approach this work with fear and reverence." Whether you're breaking the bread or receiving it, you're participating in something that spans heaven and earth, the living and the dead. You're part of the communion of saints. Come to the table with holy awe. Come believing. Come receiving with everything you have.

Try this: Whether you're leading or receiving communion next time, approach it differently. More slowly. More deliberately.

Jesus, I approach your table with reverence. I know I'm not worthy; no one is. But you've invited me anyway, and I'm accepting with fear and reverence, with faith and expectation. Help me to never approach your table casually. Help me to come with a sense of what's actually happening, that you are truly present, that this is holy ground. For those who lead communion, give them a deep sense of the weight of what they're doing. I come with holy awe, not terror but reverence. I come believing your word. I come trusting your promise. Feed me with the bread of angels. Give me what no human can give. Amen.

81

A Prayer Before Communion

When I consider your majesty, O Lord, and my own unworthiness, I tremble greatly.

—The Christian's Pattern, 1741

The Voice of the Disciple:

1. Lord, when I think about your majesty and my own unworthiness, I'm undone. Here's my problem: If I don't come to you, I'm running from life itself. But if I come without preparing my heart, I'm running straight into your displeasure. So, what do I do? You're my God. My helper. Tell me.
2. Teach me how to prepare. Show me how to get my heart ready to receive you well, whether I'm coming to the table as a worshiper or leading others there.

This short chapter captures the impossible tension every Christian feels when approaching communion: "If I don't come to you, I flee from life. And if I thrust myself in unworthily, I run into your displeasure." We feel unworthy. But we also know we need what only Christ can give. The answer is grace, not worthiness. You come, not because you're worthy but because Christ invites you. You approach, not with presumption but with humility.

Different traditions answer this differently, but here are some practices that cross denominational lines. *Confession:* Before communion, honestly name your sins to God or to a trusted friend or minister. Get clear about where you've fallen short. *Examination:* Ask yourself the questions Paul suggests in 1 Corinthians 11. Am I taking this seriously? Am I coming in faith? Am I at peace with my brothers and sisters? *Anticipation:* Come expecting something. Open your hands. Open your heart. Ask God to meet you here. And remember, the goal isn't to be perfect before you come; it's to *come honestly, humbly, and expectantly*. The table is where sinners receive grace. That's the whole point.

Try this: Before your next communion, confess one specific sin. Not in general, specifically. Then come to the table.

Lord, I'm caught in the tension. If I don't come to you, I'm running from life. But if I come unworthily, I'm running into your displeasure. So, teach me. Show me how to prepare my heart. Teach me how to approach your table with the right posture, not casual, not presumptuous, but humble and expectant. I want to receive you well. I want to come with a prepared heart. Help me confess what needs to be confessed, examine what needs to be examined, and open what needs to be opened. Then come to me. Meet me at the table. Give me what I need. Amen.

82

Examining Your Conscience and Resolving to Amend

Above all things, approach to celebrate and receive this sacrament with great humility of heart and lowly reverence.

—*The Christian's Pattern, 1741*

The Voice of Christ:

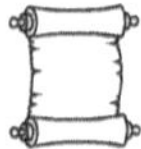

1. Come to this sacrament with deep humility, genuine faith, and honest intention. Examine your conscience carefully. Confess and repent. Don't let unaddressed sin weigh on you. Grieve not just your big failures but the daily ones. And if you have time, lay out before God every way your desires have led you astray.
2. Be honest about where you still fall short, still so caught up in the world, so driven by physical appetite, so careless with what you let in through your eyes and ears, so easily lost in fantasy, so pulled toward the external and so neglectful of the internal, so quick to laugh and so slow to be moved, so eager for comfort and so reluctant to push yourself, so hungry for news and novelty, so slow to embrace anything humble, always wanting more and tight-fisted in giving, careless with your words and unwilling to be quiet, impatient, distracted in worship, quick to check out and slow to engage, easily angered, ready to take offense, quick to judge and harsh when you correct others, cheerful when life is easy and fragile

when it's not, and always planning to do better and so rarely following through.

3. Once you've honestly confessed all of this—with real sorrow, not just guilt—make a firm decision to actually change. Then offer yourself completely to God, holding nothing back, committing everything you are and everything you have to His name.
4. There's no better offering, no more powerful blow against sin, than offering yourself fully to God at this table. If you do what you can and truly repent, then every time you come for pardon and grace, God says, "I don't want the wicked to die; I want them to turn and live." Your sins will be forgotten. All of them. They will all be forgiven.

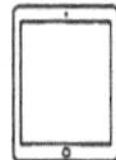

This chapter is one of the most brutally honest passages in the entire book, a litany of human weakness. That last line of passage 2 hits hard; "So often purposing many good things and yet bringing so little to effect." We plan to do better. We resolve to change. We promise God we'll be different. And then... nothing.

The chapter is about examining your conscience before communion. Specifically. Honestly. Like going to the doctor, you don't hide your symptoms. The progression is examine yourself, confess and lament, resolve to amend, and offer yourself completely to God.

Then comes the promise: "As often as they come to me for pardon and grace, I will no longer remember their sins." This is the gospel. You come honestly. You're forgiven. So, before you come to the table, examine your conscience. Ask, Where have I been cold? Where have I been distracted? And bring it all to Jesus. That's what the table is for.

Try this: Use the list in this chapter as a pre-communion examination. Read it slowly. Be honest. Then come.

Jesus, I'm examining my conscience, and I don't like what I see. I'm still so worldly, purposing many good things and bringing so little to effect. I confess all of this to you. I'm coming to you honestly, not hiding, not minimizing, and not pretending. I'm bringing all of it. I offer myself to you now, body and soul. Do in me what I can't do for myself. Forgive my sins. Restore my soul. Give me the grace to actually change. I trust your promise that as often as I come to you for pardon and grace, you will forgive. So, I'm coming. Receive me. Amen.

83

The Offering of Christ on the Cross and Our Surrender to God

As I willingly offered myself to God the Father for your sins on the cross, so ought you in the Mass willingly to offer yourself to me.

—The Christian's Pattern, 1741

The Voice of Christ:

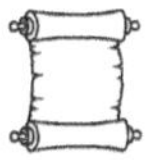

1. I gave myself completely to the Father for you, arms wide open, holding nothing back, everything offered. That's what I'm asking from you; give yourself to me the same way. Not your gifts. Not your service. You. Whatever else you bring me means nothing if you're keeping yourself back.
2. It's not enough to give me everything except yourself, just as having everything except me would never be enough for you. I gave my body and blood so that I could be fully yours and you could be fully mine. But if you hold back, that union stays incomplete. So, give yourself to God first, before anything else. This is exactly why so few people ever experience the deep freedom and inward light that's available; they can't let go of themselves. My word is clear: whoever won't give everything can't be my disciple. If you want to follow me, give me you.

This chapter gets to the heart of what's happening in communion: an exchange. Christ offers Himself completely to you. You offer yourself completely back. "I offered myself wholly to the Father for you so that I might be wholly yours and you wholly mine." That's the gift.

"Whatever you give me besides yourself doesn't concern me; I don't seek your gift but you." God doesn't want your religious activities if you're holding back the one thing He wants: you.

When you take the bread, are you saying, "Lord, I receive you"? And when you put it down, are you saying, "Lord, I give myself to you"? That's the exchange. That's what makes communion transformative instead of routine.

Try this: At your next communion, consciously offer yourself; don't just receive. Say it internally: "Here I am. All of me."

Jesus, you offered yourself completely to the Father for me. You held nothing back. Now I'm offering myself to you, completely, freely, and without reservation. I confess I've been holding back. I've wanted your blessings without your lordship and your help without your control. But you're saying, "Give me yourself." So here I am. Take me. Use me. Make me wholly yours. I want the perfect union you're describing, you wholly mine, and I wholly yours. I give you my body, my soul, my plans, my rights, my control. Everything. Make me fully yours. Amen.

84

We Should Offer Ourselves and All That Is Ours to God and Pray for Everyone

Lord, all things in heaven and earth are yours. I desire to offer myself to you as a free offering and to remain yours forever.

—The Christian's Pattern, 1741

The Voice of the Disciple:

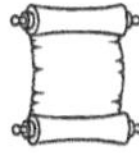

1. Lord, everything belongs to you, heaven, earth, all of it. So, I offer myself to you as a free gift to be your servant forever. Receive me alongside your own precious body with the angels as unseen witnesses. Let this be for my salvation and for the sake of everyone I love.
2. I offer you every sin and failure from the very beginning of my life until right now. Burn them away with the fire of your love. Wipe the record clean. Restore the grace I've squandered. Forgive everything. Receive this prayer.
3. What else can I do with my sin except keep confessing it and keep asking for mercy? Forgive me, God, for your name's sake, not mine. You redeemed my soul with your blood. I surrender myself into your hands. Do with me what your goodness says, not what my failures deserve.
4. I offer you the good I have too, though it's small and flawed. Refine it. Make it something you can use. And bring me, slow and unproductive as I am, to a good end.

5. I offer you the needs of everyone I love, family, friends, and all those close to me. Give them grace, comfort, and protection.
6. And I offer prayers especially for those who have hurt me, slandered me, or let me down and for everyone I've hurt in return. Forgive all of us. Clear away the suspicion, the anger, and the unresolved friction between us. Have mercy on everyone who needs it. Make us worthy of your grace and bring us all home. Amen.

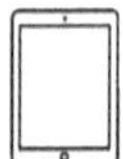

When we come to communion, we're not just receiving; we're offering. We offer ourselves in total surrender. We offer our sins through honest confession. We offer our good works; even our best efforts are flawed, but we offer them anyway. And we offer prayers for others, including enemies: "I offer to you prayers especially for those who have hurt, grieved, or slandered me." This is radical.

So, when you come to communion, remember you're not just receiving. You're offering. Offer yourself. Offer your sins. Offer prayers for those you love and for those you struggle to love. That's the full picture of what's happening at the table.

Try this: At your next communion, bring someone with you in prayer, someone who needs God's grace right now.

Lord, I'm offering myself to you today as a free offering. Receive me. I offer to you all my sins; burn them away with the fire of your love. I offer to you all the good I have, though it's little and imperfect; sanctify it and make it pleasing to you. I offer to you the needs of my parents, friends, family, and all those dear to me; let them find help, consolation, and protection in you. And I offer prayers especially for those who have hurt me and for those I've hurt; forgive us all. Heal our relationships. Have mercy on all who need your mercy. Make us worthy of your grace. Amen.

85

Holy Communion Should Not Be Lightly Neglected

You must often have recourse to the fountain of grace and divine mercy that you may be healed of your passions.

—*The Christian's Pattern, 1741*

The Voice of Christ:

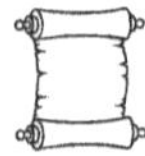

1. Keep coming back to the fountain of grace and mercy, to the source of all goodness and purity, so your old patterns can be broken, and you can be made stronger against the enemy's attacks. The enemy knows exactly what happens to people at this table. That's why he works so hard to keep them away.
2. Some people face their worst spiritual attacks right when they're preparing for communion. That's not a coincidence. The enemy comes to make you fearful and confused, to shrink your expectation, or to get you to skip it altogether. Don't listen to him. Laugh at him. Don't let his noise keep you from the table.
3. Others stay away because they're chasing a certain feeling, or they're anxious about whether they've confessed everything properly. Don't let anxiety run the show. Lay it down. Go to confession. Forgive anyone who's wronged you. Ask forgiveness where you need to. God will meet you there.
4. What's the point of putting it off? Deal with it now. Get to the table. You'll be better for it, guaranteed. Every day you

delay, it gets harder to come back. Spiritual dullness sets in fast when you stay away.

5. Sad but true, some people deliberately avoid communion so they won't feel obligated to live differently afterward. How little they love. How weak a grip on what's actually being offered. The person who lives honestly before God, always ready to receive Him, they have a blessed life. If you have a genuine reason to abstain sometimes, fine. But if it's just spiritual laziness, shake it off and come.
6. And when something genuinely prevents you from coming to the table, keep the intention alive. Approach Christ spiritually every day, calling His sacrifice to mind and letting love for Him be kindled fresh. That's not nothing. You can be nourished even when you can't physically be at the table.

Why do we skip communion? À Kempis identifies several reasons. Satan's attacks—you decide to go to communion and suddenly everything goes sideways. The enemy knows what happens at the table. Waiting for the right feelings—we think we need to feel spiritual enough, but that's not how grace works. Anxiety about confession. And procrastination—we'll deal with this later.

The remedy is to cleanse yourself quickly, make haste to take the sacrament. Come often. Come regularly. Don't wait until you feel ready. Stop letting the enemy keep you away.

Try this: If you've been skipping communion, stop. Go this week. Show up. The enemy has kept you away long enough.

Jesus, I confess I've neglected communion. I've made excuses, waited for the right feelings, or put it off. Forgive me for treating what you've given as something I can take or leave. I'm done waiting. I'm done being anxious about confession. I'm done procrastinating. I'm coming now. Help me order my life so I'm always prepared to receive you. Even when I can't physically take communion, help me approach you spiritually, calling to mind your passion and being kindled with love for you. Feed me. Strengthen me. Don't let me be kept from your table. Amen.

86

Longing for Union with Christ in Communion

Who will give me this, to find thee alone and to open my whole heart to thee?

—The Christian's Pattern, 1741

The Voice of the Disciple:

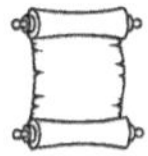

1. Lord, give me this one thing: to find you alone, to open my whole heart to you, and to enjoy you the way my soul longs to. I want to be wholly united with you, my heart withdrawn from everything else and, through coming to communion again and again, to learn more and more to love heavenly things above earthly ones. When will I be completely swallowed up in you, forgetful of myself? You in me, and I in you, together, as one.

2. You are my beloved, the best of all, the one my soul wants to stay close to every day of my life. You are my peace. In you is true rest; without you is nothing but struggle and heartache. You make your home with the humble and honest of heart. Your Spirit graciously feeds your children with the bread that comes down from heaven. No one else has a God this close to them.

3. What other people on earth are as privileged as those who follow Christ? Who is more loved than the soul that God Himself comes to feed? This is grace beyond words. This is love beyond comprehension. What can I possibly give

back? Only one thing: my whole heart, given completely to God. When that happens, when my soul is fully united to Him, He says, "If you will be with me, I will be with you." And I answer, "Stay with me, Lord. I will gladly be with you." This is my whole desire: that my heart may be united to you.

This chapter is about holy desire, longing for deeper communion with Christ. À Kempis prays, "Who will give me this, Lord, to find you alone, and open my whole heart to you?" It's the cry of someone who has tasted God's presence and wants more. The more you taste Christ in communion, the more you want Him.

Communion satisfies your hunger, but it also makes you hungrier. It gives you rest but makes you restless for more. "Truly, you're my peace maker, in whom is great peace and true rest, without whom is labor and sorrow and infinite misery." Christ gives you peace but also makes you long for the peace of heaven, where the union is complete.

The chapter ends with a beautiful exchange: "Then He will say to me, If you will be with me, I will be with you." God's not playing hard to get. He wants to be with us as much as we want to be with Him. "It is my whole desire that my heart may be united to you." Make that your prayer before communion. And watch what God does.

Try this: Before your next communion, pray just this: "This is my whole desire: that my heart may be united to you."

Jesus, I want more of you. Not just more blessings or answers to prayer. More of you. I want to find you alone, open my whole heart to you, and be swallowed up in you. You in me, and I in you. Help me, through often receiving communion, to learn more and more to relish heavenly things. You are my peace maker. In you is great peace and true rest. Without you is labor and sorrow and infinite misery. Remain with me. Be with me. And I will gladly be with you. This is my whole desire: that my heart may be united to you. Amen.

87

The Fervent Desire of Devout People to Receive Communion

O how great is thy goodness, Lord, which thou hast laid up for them that fear thee!

—The Christian's Pattern, 1741

The Voice of the Disciple:

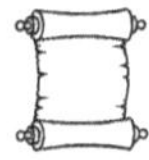

1. Lord, your goodness is so great, and you've stored it up for those who come to you in awe and need. When I think of people I know who come to communion with their whole hearts, tears streaming, on fire with love for you, I'm ashamed of how cold and flat I come. I show up dry. Unmoved. Not set on fire the way those devoted souls are. Be merciful to me, Jesus, merciful and gracious. Give me, at least sometimes, something of your tender, heartfelt love. Strengthen my faith. Increase my hope. Set my love on fire and keep it burning.
2. Your mercy, Lord, can give me the grace I'm asking for; you can visit me with a spirit of fervor when it pleases you. I don't burn with the great desires of those who are wholly devoted to you. But by your grace, I want to have that ardent desire. I'm reaching for it. I want to be counted among your fervent lovers.

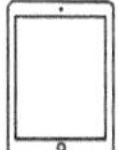

This chapter addresses something most of us have felt: comparing our spiritual experience to others and feeling inadequate. À Kempis looks at devout people who come to communion with tears and burning hearts and says, "I'm confounded and blush within myself." He's dry while others are on fire.

He doesn't give up. He prays for the desire he doesn't have that his faith may be strengthened, his hope increased, and his love set on fire. He's not asking for emotional highs; he's asking for genuine transformation.

"Though I burn not with so great desires as those singularly devoted to you, yet by your grace, I desire to have this great, ardent desire." Desire the desire. Trust that when it pleases God, He will visit you with that spirit of fervor.

Try this: Come to the table this week even if you don't feel it. Desire the desire. That's enough to start.

Jesus, to be honest, I feel dry and cold and flat when I come to your table. Others seem moved. I feel nothing. But you're merciful. Be merciful to me now. Not because I deserve it, but because you're merciful. I want to be like those devout people who long after you with their whole heart. I want my faith strengthened, my hope increased, and my love set on fire. By your grace, give me the desire I don't have. Even if it's just a taste. Fan the flame. Visit me with the spirit of fervor. Amen.

88

Devotion Is Obtained Through Humility and Self-Surrender

You ought to seek the grace of devotion fervently, to ask it earnestly, to expect it patiently.

—The Christian's Pattern, 1741

The Voice of the Beloved:

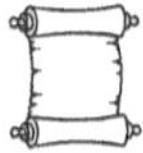

1. Seek devotion eagerly. Ask for it persistently. Wait for it patiently and with confidence. When it comes, receive it with gratitude, hold it with humility, work hard with it, and trust God to decide when and how His grace visits you. Above all, humble yourself when you feel little or no devotion, but don't spiral into despair. God often gives in a moment what He's held back for a long time. He sometimes gives at the end what He delayed at the beginning of prayer.
2. Sometimes it's something small blocking grace from getting through, though calling it small hardly does it justice when it's keeping out something this good. Remove it and what you've been longing for will come. The moment you hand yourself over to God with your whole heart, not seeking your own way, not insisting on your own preferences, but fixing yourself entirely on Him, you'll find yourself at peace. Nothing satisfies quite like what satisfies God's will.
3. Then something opens up. You see clearly. You're satisfied. You stand in wonder, heart expanded, because the hand of the Lord is on you, and you've given yourself to Him

completely. Blessed is the person who seeks God with everything they have and doesn't waste their soul on empty things. This person comes to communion not for feelings or personal comfort but for one reason: God's honor and glory. And paradoxically, that's when they receive everything they were looking for.

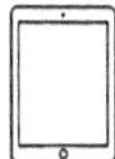

What do you do when you don't feel it? Humble yourself but don't despair. When you feel dry and flat inside, don't perform devotion you don't have. Don't beat yourself up either. Just stay humble, stay present, and trust that God sees you.

God often gives in a moment what He's held back for a long time. Sometimes He gives at the very end what He seemed to be withholding all along. And sometimes it's something small standing between you and grace, some tiny area of stubbornness or some habit you haven't surrendered. It seems insignificant. But it's blocking something enormous.

The solution is total surrender: The moment you hand yourself over to God with your whole heart, you find yourself at peace. This person isn't at the table for what they can get. They're at the table for God's glory. And paradoxically, that's when they get everything they were looking for.

Try this: Identify one thing you're holding back from God. Surrender it at the table. Not after, at the table.

God, I'm not feeling it right now. I come to your table, and I feel dry. Empty. But you're saying, Don't despair, keep coming, stay humble. So, I'll keep showing up. I'll keep coming. Is there anything I'm holding back from you? Some little thing hindering your grace? Show me. Give me the courage to surrender it. I'm at your table, not for my own comfort or spiritual experiences. I'm here for your honor and glory. And I trust that in seeking you that way, you'll give me more than I could have asked for. Amen.

89

Laying Our Needs Before Christ and Asking for Grace

Most holy and loving Lord, I desire to receive thee with all devotion.

—The Christian's Pattern, 1741

The Voice of the Disciple:

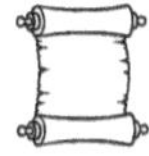

1. Lord, holy, loving, and close, you know my weakness. You know how much I'm carrying, how often I'm grieved, tempted, troubled, and worn down. I'm coming to you for help. There's no one who knows me the way you do, no one else who can truly comfort and restore me. You see exactly what I need and how spiritually poor I really am.
2. Here I am, empty-handed, calling for grace. Refresh me. Set fire to my coldness with the fire of your love. Clear my blurry vision with the brightness of your presence. Help earthly things lose their grip on me. Lift my heart toward heaven. Don't let me wander, chasing distractions. Be the one thing that satisfies from now on. Because you alone are my food and drink, my love and my joy, my sweetness and everything I need.
3. I want your presence to set me on fire, to kindle, burn, and transform me from the inside out, until I'm made one spirit with you through the grace of deep union and the warmth of your love. Don't let me leave empty. You've dealt so mercifully with your people throughout history. Deal

with me the same way now. Is it any wonder I want to be set on fire by you and to die to myself in the process? You are a fire always burning and never going out, love that purifies the heart and clears the mind.

This chapter is about radical honesty with God before communion. À Kempis lays it all out: "You know my weakness. How many evils I'm oppressed by, how often I'm grieved, tempted, troubled, and defiled." No pretending. No religious masks. Just, "I'm a mess. I need you."

Not "I come to show you how spiritual I am," just "I need you. I'm desperate. Help me." That's the right posture at the table. And notice what he asks for: not just feelings but transformation. "Set fire to my coldness. Enlighten my blindness. Be the only sweet thing to me from now on." Change what I desire. Help me desire you more than anything else.

"You alone are my food and drink, my love and my joy." We're not just receiving a symbol; we're receiving Him. Come hungry. Come cold. Come needy. Because that's what the table is for.

Try this: Come to your next communion with nothing polished to offer. Just your need. That's the whole point.

Jesus, I'm coming to your table, and I need to be honest. I'm a mess. You know my weakness, how often I'm grieved, tempted, troubled, and defiled. I'm coming because I have nowhere else to go. Refresh me. Set fire to my coldness. Enlighten my blindness. Don't let me wander, distracted by earthly things. Be the only sweet thing to me from now on. You alone are my food and drink, my love and my joy, my sweetness and all my good. Set me on fire. Transform me. Feed me. I'm yours. Amen.

90

Fervent Love and Passionate Desire to Receive Christ

With great devotion and burning love, with the affection and fervor of my whole heart, I desire to receive thee, Lord.

—The Christian's Pattern, 1741

The Voice of the Disciple:

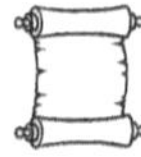

1. With deep devotion and burning love, with the full passion and longing of my heart, I want to receive you, Lord, the way the saints and devout people throughout history have received you. The ones who were closest to you, the most fervent in their love. My God, my everlasting love, my whole good, my never-ending joy, I would gladly receive you with the most passionate desire and worthy reverence any saint has ever had.
2. Even though I'm not there yet—I don't have all those feelings, all that burning devotion—I offer you the whole longing of my heart, as if all the desire of every devoted soul were mine to give. Everything a holy mind can imagine and want, I offer to you with the greatest reverence and inward affection. I want to hold nothing back. Freely, willingly, myself and everything that is mine, I give to you.
3. My Lord God, my Creator and my Redeemer, I want to receive you today with affection, reverence, praise, and honor. With gratitude, faith, hope, and purity. The way your mother, Mary, received the news of your coming,

humbly and devoutly, saying, "I am the Lord's servant. Let it be done to me according to your word."

4. And like John the Baptist, who leaped for joy in his mother's womb at your presence and who later stood before you humbling himself, saying, "The friend of the bridegroom rejoices greatly at the bridegroom's voice," I want to be on fire with great and holy longing and to offer myself to you with everything I have.

5. I bring you the praises and gratitude of every devoted heart, the love of every holy mind, all the thanksgiving, honor, and devotion that any creature has ever offered you. I invite every heavenly being and every devoted follower to give thanks with me and to praise you. Let every person, tribe, and tongue magnify your name with the highest joy and most fervent devotion. Let all who come reverently to your table find grace and mercy, and let them pray for me, a sinner. When they've received their desired devotion and joyful union, when they leave your table well fed and deeply renewed, may they think of me too. Because we come to this table together and we leave together—one body, united in you. All thanks and glory to you, Lord Jesus. Amen.

This is the final chapter of Book Four, a crescendo of desire. À Kempis throws everything into this prayer, reaching for the devotion of all the saints, the passion of Mary, and the joy of John the Baptist leaping in the womb.

"Although I be unworthy to have all those feelings of devotion, yet I offer to you the whole affection of my heart, as if I alone had all those kindled desires." You bring what you have. The heart's intention counts. Come with desire. Come holding nothing back. Desire Christ passionately. Receive Him gratefully. Remember each other humbly.

Try this: Pray for someone else at the table this week. And when you leave, carry them with you.

Jesus, I want to receive you the way the saints received you. I know my desire is weak, and my devotion is cold. But I'm offering you what I have: the whole affection of my heart, as if it were as fervent as the greatest saint's. I want to receive you today with affection, reverence, praise, and honor and with gratitude, faith, hope, and purity. I want to say with Mary, "Behold the handmaid of the Lord; let it be done to me according to your word." And when others come to your table today, may they be pleased to remember me. And I will remember them. For we come to this table together, members of one body, united in you. All thanks and glory to you, Lord Jesus. Amen.

Epilogue

A Benediction for the Journey

If you've made it this far, you've walked a long road with Thomas à Kempis and John Wesley. You've been invited into deep water. And if the Holy Spirit has been at work, you're not the same person who opened the first page.

Book One asked you to examine your life honestly. What are you really living for? Not what you say you're living for, but what your actual choices reveal. Book Two called you inward. Stop performing Christianity for an audience and start cultivating genuine intimacy with Christ. The inner life isn't about feeling spiritual; it's about staying close to the One who is the source of all life. Book Three gave you language for the hard times. When comfort vanishes, when God feels distant, when everything goes dark, you're not abandoned. You're being formed. Book Four brought you to the table. Holy Communion isn't a ritual to endure or a bonus feature for the especially devout. It's food for the journey. Christ Himself comes to you there to forgive, to strengthen, to transform, and to unite.

Here's what I've learned in my own fumbling attempts to live this way: You can't do all of it at once. You'll try. You'll fail. You'll feel overwhelmed. And that's okay. Pick one thing. Just one. Maybe it's carving out fifteen minutes of silence each morning to practice the presence of God. Maybe it's examining your conscience before bed each night. Maybe it's coming to communion as often as you can with actual preparation and expectation. Maybe it's the brutal honesty of asking yourself once a week, What am I really living for?

The Methodist movement started with people gathering in small groups, asking each other hard questions: How is it with your soul? Where did you see God this week? Where did you fall short? They held each other accountable, not to rules but to relationship, to the ongoing work of becoming people who actually love God and love their neighbors. This book isn't meant to be read once and shelved. It's meant to be lived with. Come back to it. Let it read you. Let it expose what needs exposing. Let it invite you into what's possible.

As Pete Greig says, "Prayer must outwork itself in action… it is about the saying of prayers for sure, but also the becoming of prayers in a thousand practical ways."[1] Start there. Start small. Start today.

Jesus, I've heard your voice in these pages. Now give me the courage to respond. I don't want to be a hearer only; I want to be a doer. I don't want to just know about the spiritual life; I want to live it. Give me grace for the failures. Give me your presence, always. Make me a person of deep spirituality and practical holiness. Form Christ in me. Use me for your glory. And when I get to the end of my journey, let me say with my whole heart, "It was worth it." You were worth it. Amen.

1. Greig, Pete. Dirty Glory: Go Where Your Best Prayers Take You. NavPress, 2016.

SCAN HERE to learn more about Invite Ministries—created to invite people to a deeper faith and living relationship with Jesus Christ

www.ingramcontent.com/pod-product-compliance
Lightning Source LLC
Chambersburg PA
CBHW020915060726
47591CB00004B/1252
9781971591001